D1032784

Mabel Dodge Luhan

Twayne's United States Authors Series

David J. Nordloh, Editor
Indiana University, Bloomington

TUSAS 477

Mabel Dodge Luhan in Taos,
New Mexico, during her mature years.
Photograph courtesy of Rowena Meyers Martinez.

Mabel Dodge Luhan

By Winifred L. Frazer

University of Florida

Twayne Publishers • Boston

LIBRARY
COLBY-SAWYER COLLEGE
NEW LONDON, N.H. 03257

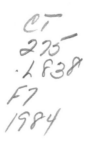

CT
275
.L838
F7
1984

1/85

Mabel Dodge Luhan

Winifred L. Frazer

Copyright © 1984 by G. K. Hall & Company
All Rights Reserved
Published by Twayne Publishers
A Division of G. K. Hall & Company
70 Lincoln Street
Boston, Massachusetts 02111

Permission to reprint the poem
"False Start" is granted by John
Nims, editor of *Poetry.*

Book Production by Elizabeth Todesco

Book Design by Barbara Anderson

Printed on permanent/durable acid-free
paper and bound in the United States
of America.

Library of Congress Cataloging in Publication Data

Frazer, Winifred L., 1916-
    Mabel Dodge Luhan.

    (Twayne's United States authors series; TUSAS 477)
    Bibliography: p. 115
    Includes index.
    1. Luhan, Mabel Dodge, 1879–1962.
    2. Intellectuals--United States--Biography.
I. Title.   II. Series.
CT275.L838F7   1984   973.9'092'4 [B]   84-10839
ISBN 0-8057-7418-1

95986

Contents

About the Author

Winifred (Loesch) Frazer grew up in Colorado. She received her B.A. from the University of Wisconsin, her M.A. from the University of Maine, and, after attending graduate school at the University of Minnesota, her Ph.D. from the University of Florida, where she was a member of the faculty for twenty-six years.

Now professor emeritus, she has taught courses in various areas of American literature and written on Eugene O'Neill and twentieth-century American drama. Her published works include *The Theme of Loneliness in Modern American Drama* (Dusenbury), *Love as Death in "The Iceman Cometh," E. G. and E. G. O.: Emma Goldman and "The Iceman Cometh,"* various essays in periodicals, and the analytical "Drama" section in *American Literary Scholarship* for the five years 1976 through 1980.

Preface

It would have seemed most unlikely that the little girl who grew up in the 1880s among the wealthy families of Buffalo, New York, racing her pony cart among the cemetery paths where the prominent were buried, would eighty-three years later be buried in a lonely, neglected graveyard in Taos, New Mexico. No one could have predicted that this little girl, born on 26 February 1879 to Charles F. and Sara Cook Ganson, would, after marrying three husbands of her social class or artistic interests, spend nearly the last forty years of her life married to a Pueblo Indian. No one could have predicted either that this only child of uncongenial parents would prove a catalyst for the bringing together of radical champions of the poor, labor leaders, and political theorists, with artists, writers, and playwrights who were striving toward new forms of expression in early twentieth-century America.

Between 1904 and 1912 Mabel and Edwin Dodge attracted the best-known international celebrities from Europe and America to their Villa Curonia near Florence, Italy. There, with only occasional visits to New York, London, and Paris, they lived and held open house, providing a meeting place for interchange among the aspiring and the accomplished in the arts. Returning to America in 1912, Mabel conducted during the next few years an even more celebrated salon on Fifth Avenue in New York, where artists and radicals congregated.

But why, one might ask, if her fame rests on her abilities as a notable hostess, is Mabel Luhan included in a series of volumes on authors of the United States? Although not formally trained as a writer and lacking the self-discipline usually required, Mabel Dodge, in the 1930s, wrote four remarkable volumes, entitled *Intimate Memories,* on her own life and experiences. Of course she included mention of the artists, radicals, and writers she had known, and thus throws light, not only on many of them, but also on the times at the end of the nineteenth century and the early decades of the twentieth. In 1932 she also wrote *Lorenzo in Taos,* her account of how she persuaded D. H. Lawrence to come to America to the ranch she gave him, and in 1935 *Winter in Taos,* recounting a day in the life of her Indian husband, Tony Luhan. In these six volumes, which describe notable characters and give a sharp picture of the times, there emerges a remarkably honest character portrayal of the writer herself. The great interest in the new art (or science) of psychoanalysis during the years of Mabel's youth and maturity is illustrated in her acute and telling practice of it in relating her own life's story. Any reader interested in American literature during the early years of the century may, therefore, with various purposes in mind, want to read one or more of the six autobiographical volumes of Mabel Luhan.

To be included in an authors' series, however, a writer must have that individual style that is unique. Here too, Mabel Luhan qualifies. As one greatly interested in the visual and tactile arts of painting, sculpture, and architecture, as well as in the linguistic arts of drama, poetry, and fiction, she vividly portrays herself, her friends, and her times. Particularly interested in home decoration, she describes the elegant settings of her Italian and New York salons as well as the simple pueblo-style houses she built in Taos. She has a good eye for color and form, and a unique perspective on the friends who visited the homes she created. These, and an unusual honesty about herself, qualify her work to fit the definition of literature as an art which provides the reader both profit and pleasure.

Winifred L. Frazer

University of Florida

Chronology

1917   Marries Maurice Sterne at Peekskill, New York.

1917–1918 Arthur Brisbane pays $30 apiece for articles for *New York Journal,* syndicated in all Hearst papers from 13 August 1917 through 8 February 1918. The Sternes move to Taos, New Mexico. Mabel visits the Indian pueblo near Taos, teaches Indian women knitting and sewing. Builds house in Taos. Meets Tony (Antonio) Lujan. Encourages Maurice to go back to New York— later gets divorce.

1922   Persuades D. H. Lawrence and wife to settle in Taos.

1923   Marries Tony Lujan (Luhan) in Taos.

1925   Frieda Lawrence sends Mabel original manuscript of *Sons and Lovers,* in payment for gift of ranch.

1932   *Lorenzo in Taos.*

1933   *Background,* volume 1 of *Intimate Memories.*

1935   *European Experiences,* volume 2 of memoirs. *Winter in Taos.*

1936   *Movers and Shakers,* volume 3 of *Intimate Memories.*

1937   *Edge of Taos Desert,* volume 4.

1948   *Taos and Its Artists.*

1962   Mabel Luhan dies in Taos, 13 August.

Chapter One
Early Life in Victorian Buffalo: *Intimate Memories: Background*

Girlhood and Family

From the distant perspective of a white-walled adobe house in Taos, New Mexico, Mabel Dodge Luhan in *Background* (1933) looks back nostalgically upon Buffalo, New York, the place of her birth more than fifty years before. Calling it "a cozy town," she begins her first of four autobiographical volumes of *Intimate Memories* with a dedication to the Buffalo of the years 1879 to 1900, when she lived and grew to womanhood.[1]

Admitting that her view of the city was limited, she does not describe the industrial part of Buffalo, the great port and railroad center across the tracks, or the people who lived there. Her world included the fashionable part of the city, where families of wealth owned mansions, through whose walls almost no rumble of the outside world intruded. In the first chapter, "Our Town," she presents an image of her neighborhood like Thornton Wilder's romantic view of the small town of Grovers Corners, New Hampshire, in his play of the same title. Although half a century later she recognizes the limitations of the life in that time and place, she extols its virtues. "My childhood," she writes, "had a wild, sweet, enthralling zestfulness," and this in spite of the fact that she was not happy. According to the memories she details of her life as an only child of unresponsive and uncongenial parents, one wonders that she did not look back on her town with sorrow rather than with joyful nostalgia.

Perhaps it says something about the art of autobiography that skillful evocation of the past causes the author to experience pleasure in spite of the pain of the events. Mabel describes her surroundings and her own reactions in details which bring one social level of Victorian Buffalo vividly to life. Interest in her first volume of memoirs lies not in trying to evaluate its historical coverage nor, as in later volumes, in her assessment of the celebrities she knew, but in the memorable picture of a rich girl at the end of the nineteenth century as she paints it during the early 1930s.

Of the house she lived in, she writes, "The rooms were filled with furniture that had no significance for me." Telling of "the ache and the hunger" in her, she continues, "I believe if there had been one picture in that house . . . from which I could have drawn some spirit of life, I would have been satisfied by it. . . . Or one face that had real feeling in it for me would have answered. But there was nothing and no one" (21). To allay her loneliness, she used to press her lips against the Mother Goose wallpaper in her room, hoping for a response from the pink and blue figures.

Her mother was as unsympathetic a figure to her as was the house, which to the little girl belonged to her mother alone. She describes her mother as "proud and independent," with an "arrogant, high-bridged nose" that resembled "a narrow curving beak." Since Sara Ganson had no intellectual interests to engage her mind, she ran the household with great rigidity, enforced the strictest rules on the maids, and treated her daughter with cold impersonality as a fixture of the place. According to Mabel, "She had no imagination and no fear and she seemed to live without love."

Her father was apparently even more unresponsive to Mabel, if that was possible. She describes him as a man "whose years passed in an increasing torment and whose temper grew worse with the years." Their social set had since his youth accepted him as a "crank," so that even if he lost his temper at a formal dinner party, threw a plate to the floor, and stalked from the room, he was not ostracized. According to Mabel, he hated his wife and made no attempt to conceal his feeling, hoisting his monogrammed flag up the flagpole on the front lawn whenever she went to visit Mabel's Grandma Cook, flying it all the time she was away, and at half-mast the day she returned. Mabel implies that he needed psychological help, which at that time was not available. When he was extraordinarily angry in the morning, he would stalk to his downtown office at a rapid pace, arrogantly passing most of the walkers and even some of the carriages and saying good morning to no one. According to Mabel's memory, he was never pleasant to anyone except after a serious attack of gout or inflammatory rheumatism; he would curse those who nursed him, but afterward would emerge from his room with a serene face. "What a pity," she writes, that it took such suffering "to give him a short respite from the inner dragon!" (117).

Worst of all for a child, perhaps, was that her father paid no attention to her, even brushing past her in the hall with "a look of dislike." Since he smoked strong cigars, she grew up to hate the smell in any house as long as she lived. Apparently both his wife and his mother, who lived only four blocks away in the same neighborhood, took his outbursts of temper with equanimity. When he would jam his hat on his head and rush to Grandma Ganson's house, she would welcome him to his old room upstairs. It was not long, however, before he would stamp down again, complaining of the plumbing, and return to his own home. To the child, however, it was sad to have a parent to whom she was at best a nonentity. Although she dreamed of a romantic father who had been in strange countries and brought back "turquoise beads strung on a string," these remained in a drawer, and the only father she knew was the one who treated her so unfeelingly as a nuisance.

Mabel's lifelong interest in art and architecture was perhaps forecast by her childish delight in the gift of a simple paint box. Perceptive concerning color, even as a child, she can remember her frustration at not being able to get distinctive shades: "Vermillion was never sharp enough"; "the blues were common, even when I mixed them myself"; "carmine was a full, real color but not a very uplifting one, to my feeling." Also, she felt such a compulsion to stay within the lines of the picture she was painting that it was almost like a ritualistic death if her paints slopped over the line, as when she feared stepping on the cracks of the sidewalk. Whether or not she married an architect and then a painter because of her early artistic abilities and interest, she was stimulated by the professions of these men and in turn contributed to their development. She was designing houses, decorating apartments, and creating costumes for herself throughout her entire life, and part of her attraction for so many different celebrities was no doubt the pleasing surroundings in which she lived.

Mabel's description of the decoration of the "dead" Victorian Ganson house perhaps clarifies why, when she grew up and could create her own, she emphasized simplicity and light. As she remembered it, no one really lived in the house. Her mother drove out shopping and calling most of the day, and her father, if he was home, retreated to his own room upstairs. She and Mary Ann, her nurse, after walking in the afternoons, would sit at one of the windows, looking out at the passersby, finding much more life there than inside the house. The furniture of the rooms consisted of sets of thick upholstery trimmed with cord-and-ball fringes. Heavy, ornate curtains and dreary pictures added to Mabel's depression: one was of "a stormy dark-green sea with a faint blob of light in the distance . . . in a gold frame that had a great many bulging moldings." As she grew older, she concluded that the grandfather clock with the picture above its face of "three ships rocking back and forth on a stormy sea" symbolized the three members of the Ganson family, tossing about in isolated misery in the Victorian mansion.

As to pictures, Mabel remembers the walls as covered with all kinds of pictures of animals. One showed mounted horses charging into battle, straining forward with one desperate white charger at the head. Others showed racing horses or champion dogs, one a painting of their Boston bulldog who had died. Mabel notes that although none of the Gansons loved each other nor anyone outside the family, they all three loved animals. Indeed, if she can be believed, her mother would pet and caress and talk to Jack, the brown Irish terrier, while completely neglecting Mabel; and her father's attentions to Moxie, the blue Skye terrier, were kinder than those he gave to her. So overwhelming was the family's affection for their pets that Mabel, writing in middle age, can remember them more vividly than any of the servants or neighbors. And so "the many heavy months and years" went by, while Mabel, unable to reconcile herself to so much unhappiness, "tried to plot" her way out of it.

On her mother's side Mabel was descended from Constant Cook, younger son of a family in Surrey, England, who received a grant of land from the king and settled in Bath, New York. His son, Mabel's grandfather, married Mary McKay, whose father had also come from England. They had four daughters, considered great beauties, with clear white skin, blue eyes, and auburn hair, one of whom, Sara, became Mabel's mother. Mabel recalled her Grandfather Cook as being very tall and very slender, with broad shoulders and a square white beard. Since he seemed to spend all his time in mental speculation, she rarely heard him speak or smile, but she greatly admired his aloof grandeur. In the small town of Bath, he dominated the bank, the courthouse, and much of the business, from the construction of houses and stores to the building of railroads. His high-bridged nose and arched drooping eyelids made him look like an American eagle, young Mabel thought. Once when, with his bony thin hand, he presented her ceremoniously with a silver dollar, Mabel felt awe at this solemn moment, but also a sense of the ridiculous that an old man should so worship a dollar and make a sacrament of it. How she wished he might have feeling for other symbols of the good life! But business interested him more than human emotions or the arts or the affection of a little granddaughter.

Finding the town of Bath restrictive, the Cooks moved to New York City, where they built a large house on their Fifth Avenue property, which was almost across the street from the Metropolitan Museum. The obelisk at the museum dominated the scene through the second-story windows of the house. In spite of its view of Central Park and its cream-colored stone and marble walls nearly covered with vines, still Mabel saw this elegant dwelling as a mausoleum, in which the ritualized lives of her grandparents never varied: her grandfather came home from Wall Street each day in his high silk hat; her grandmother came in from her drive in the park. Neither spoke much, and both retired to a life of their own until dinner in the majestic dining room, where food took on an importance beyond that of sustenance for the body. It was a dull household for a child to visit.

Mabel's memories of her grandparents, however, were still vivid at the time she wrote of them nearly fifty years later. She describes the pride she felt in accompanying her tall, straight grandfather, elegantly dressed in white waistcoat, cutaway, and striped trousers, to St. Thomas's Church: "One felt like a happy, irresponsible barnacle on a noble, purposeful ship plowing her way severely to some magnificent goal, as one sat beside him in that church. He and the church were one and I was being carried along with it." Her grandfather had an air of mystical comtemplation as he passed the collection plate, an air which Mabel found suitable to a man who so worshiped the dollar. Actually, she claims, he would have found no satire in the sly interweaving of dollar signs into the Gothic carvings on the doorways during a later renovation of the church.

Mabel saw her grandmother as a cross, domineering old woman, who found fault with everything and was often in tears, through either boredom or anger. After being groomed, oiled, and powdered by her maid, she would spend the morning at her desk writing letters of advice to her four daughters and to other relatives, whom she expected to carry out her orders no matter where they lived or how old they became. Sara, Mabel's mother, obliged by writing replies full of the tiniest details of the management of her house in Buffalo. Since Grandma Cook's own house was run by an exceedingly efficient butler downstairs and a long-time housekeeper upstairs, she had plenty of time to advise others on how to care for theirs. Looking always disagreeable, she did not approve of Mabel's father, who reciprocated the feeling of animosity. Although seemingly without virtues, being "hateful to servants and to nearly every one else," still she was "herself," a trait Mabel admired in her and also in her grandfather, both of whom were "real people" (137).

Grandma Ganson's house in Buffalo, however, was a different matter. Since it was close to where she and her parents lived, this large square brick house with a cupola on top of it played an important part in Mabel's life. Grandma Ganson spent much time in a rocking chair in her bay window with its glass panes reaching to the floor. Much of the attraction of this spot was that a club for middle-aged and elderly gentlemen adjoined her lot on one side, and a club for young men (in whom her worried family felt she was too much interested) stood at the corner of the next block. Since the bay window projected far beyond the house she could see all the gentlemen who arrived at either club and eagerly responded to their polite greetings. Besides, Trinity Church was directly across the street. As a long-time member Mrs. Ganson was very familiar with all who passed inside and became immediately acquainted with any young curate who might be assigned to assist the parish. In her will, she reasonably left her house to the church for a rectory: indeed, while she lived she had considered this church with its "drawing-room atmosphere" almost an extension of her own home.

Grandma Ganson's sitting room was the one—of all those in houses Mabel knew—which seemed most compatible, perhaps because her grandmother was always there to read or talk to her. Besides, the senior Ganson house had a long banister, which as long as she wore short skirts (probably through the 1880s), Mabel loved to slide down. Although the many massive mahogany folding doors with embossed silver knobs added to the heavy feeling in the house, and the dark upholstered furniture was ugly, Mabel appreciated the fine workmanship in the former and the comfort of the latter, and the "homey sense of life" in the sitting room which was constantly used. And Grandma Ganson was so cheerful a person that the widow's black dresses which she wore became "symbols of her gayety." In contrast to the cold feeling in her own house and the remote attitude of her parents, it was a joy for Mabel to enter this "nourishing" atmosphere and to feel "secure and loose."

Summer Houses

Mabel could have been labeled a poor little rich girl, for although she seemed to lack warmth in her home, she was familiar with a great number of houses. Besides her own house in Buffalo, the senior Ganson house nearby, the Cook house in New York City, and the old family house in Bath, she spent time in a variety of fine summer houses in the places where Buffalo society emigrated. Since summer is the most beautiful time of year in that cold lake city, Mabel could not understand why, about the beginning of July, all the wealthy families departed. But such was the custom, and that in spite of the fact that the set to which her family belonged had built a club house on Falconwood Island in the Niagara River, which was not more than a two-hour boat trip from the foot of Ferry Street. Mabel remembers days there as "dreamy and peaceful," but her parents and the parents of her friends always departed for long summer stays at more distant resorts.

One place where she and her mother spent part of each summer was the old family house in Bath, which had been inherited by one of the Cook sisters, Louise, who lived there with her husband, Judge Rumsey Miller, and their four children. Besides this spacious home and their New York mansion, her Cook grandparents owned a summer house in the Berkshires, near Lenox, Massachusetts. They named it Wheatleigh after the home of their forbears in Surrey. There, in spite of not liking foreign things, they built a large Italian villa, the spacious grounds of which Mabel felt were "manicured." In the orderly greenhouses, one could only look at the still bunches of grapes on the vines, and in the stables each meticulously groomed horse stood in its own stall with its spotless tan-colored blanket bound in dark blue with the monogram H. H. C. on one flank.

Before Wheatleigh was built, the Cooks had rented a cottage during the summers in the small town of Lenox itself. Mabel looked back nostalgically to the wide shaded streets, the lanes with tall goldenrod swaying in the fall, and the sleepy town uninvaded as yet by motor cars. There she had her pony cart and pony, Cupid, whom she encouraged to run up and down the hills and through the village streets at full gallop, until discouraged by the local preacher. The love of open country and a fearlessness of being out on her own stayed with her all her life. Her move from New York to the remote New Mexico town of Taos in mid-life is not astonishing in the light of the child she was. And her antipathy for "the completely conquered landscape" of Wheatleigh makes understandable her pleasure in the open sage-brush covered land of New Mexico.

The Cooks also owned a summer place at Newport, Rhode Island, the most fashionable of resorts for wealthy New Yorkers at the turn of the century. There Mabel was fascinated with the ocean. As she stood on the promontory of her grandfather's estate with her feet in wet pock marks on the mammoth rocks, she was terrified to "look down into the mass of deep green water billowing and boiling against the resistant stone." And on blustery days, if she saw from the window a lonely figure in black oilskin fishing from the rocks, she would visualize his fate if he slipped into the "ugly, gaping waves." Although the ocean frightened Mabel, and was always "the least comprehensible, the most unavailing element," still she loved the feel of the smooth white sand, the alluring seashells, and most of all the faintly musty odor of the house.

Mabel also recalled Richfield Springs in central New York State, where her father went to drink the sulphur water and bathe in the springs. As at other "springs" that her family visited, the regimen at this one consisted of drinking the water before breakfast, eating, then bathing. Her description of the people who patronize springs suggests that Mabel was obviously not a believer in the virtue of the rotten-smelling sulphur water:

Later they bathe, lying in the water; they feel it penetrating them, removing their disorders, and all the rest of the day they are a little fatigued and a little chastened in mind by the thought that the miraculous water is coursing through them and undoing harm and changing their poisons into fine, healthy blood. They gradually assume a blessed expression—as though they had been wrestling with the Devil and had overcome him, an expression lent to them by their faith that the "cure" has made them over. (168)

Such irreverence, combined with her clear eye for details, makes Mabel an admirable commentator on the ways of the class in which she grew up.

Although Mabel remembers some of the peculiar families in her own neighborhood of Buffalo who suffered from ostracism or tragedy, she considered several normal households as unhappy as her own. It would seem that wives hated husbands, who barely tolerated their wives and who lived as separately as possible; that parents treated children coldly as products of the marriage, and as something of a nuisance; that children, always in the care of nurses and governesses or private schools, felt removed from family affection; and that each lived the proscribed and ritualized existence required by the turn-of-the-century culture of the wealthy classes in Buffalo. The picture she drew may have some truth in it. Edith Wharton in the north and Ellen Glasgow in the south, as well as Henry James from his English base, satirized the rich, whose appearance of happiness contrasted with the inner turmoil hidden by the pressures of their culture.

Schools and Teachers

Until she was sixteen Mabel attended St. Margaret's, a small girls' school housed across the street from her own house. Of academic learning, Mabel could remember only that Miss Tuck in Bible class explained that Leah's being "tender-eyed" meant either that she had gentle eyes or sore eyes. Perhaps this one fact stuck in her memory beyond all others because she could not decide whether Miss Tuck herself had tender or sore eyes, which were soft but looked as though they hurt her. Miss Tuck, whom Mabel remembered as tall and thin, a Gothic figure with a profile long "like a goat's," used daily to drop to her knees in prayer, while each girl, in the same position, was convinced that her teacher talked directly to God. After prayers, Miss Tuck was sometimes playful in returning a lost brooch to some girl or calling one to the front of the room for some compliment, but at other times, she leaned across the desk and, with tears in her eyes, chided the girls for their lack of spirit and betrayal of the standards of the school. So overwhelming were her manner and the charges she made that girls wept for the pain which Miss Tuck suffered for their misdemeanors. All day they "crept" through the schoolrooms chastened and "diminished" by the morning prayers.

Although Mabel may not have remembered learning anything at St. Margaret's, she did on two occasions at least succeed in creative endeavors, leading her teachers to think she could consistently do much better if she tried, but leaving her baffled on each occasion as to how she had succeeded. One evening she wrote a composition for Mrs. Bush—a story which seemed to write itself as it gushed out whole from her being—and the next day she was commended as having real ability. But Mabel could not recapture the formula at will, nor could she explain to herself or others how such virtuosity had occurred. She concluded that in this life one must simply learn to wait for inspiration. An even more startling incident of the same kind occurred with her art teacher, Miss Rose Clark, who had her own studio downtown and came once a week to teach the girls to paint, usually a still life. Fond as she was of the teacher, and much as she profited from her love of shades and colors and forms, Mabel never succeeded in drawing well except once, when she herself knew she had caught "the heavy ripe pear hanging at the end of its stem," which her pleased teacher praised. Miss Clark, too, could not understand why Mabel could not, with work, do the same again, but to the girl it was not through work that she had succeeded, but through some unexplained haphazard magic. Again, she decided there was nothing to do but wait for another occasion when she would be carried beyond her usual self.

In 1895 Grandmother Cook, deciding that Mabel was undisciplined at St. Margaret's, commanded that she be sent to Miss Graham's, a boarding school for young ladies on West Seventy-second Street in New York. Mrs. Cook judged that Mabel's tomboy ways would be best curbed through the deportment taught at a proper city school. Predictably, Miss Graham was another teacher who fitted the pattern: "She was tall and spare, with a primly shaped mouth, gray hair parted and crimped in metallic waves, and eyebrows that slanted upwards towards each other, giving her the expression of being always slightly annoyed" (232).

It is not strange, in view of her description of the principal (and of her sister, "a softer copy of the same thing"), that Mabel found the tall narrow schoolhouse to be a prison. In Buffalo she had had her pony cart and her bicycle and had been allowed great freedom. Now she slept in a room with two other girls, woke up feeling stuffy and depressed, and found the girls dull and uninteresting. She besieged her mother with letters begging release from the intolerable confinement of this city finishing school.

When Mrs. Ganson withdrew her at Christmas time, however, Mabel did regret leaving one friend who influenced her future life.

Although she had learned nothing from the school itself, she had nevertheless come under the influence of a lonely, friendless American girl, who, having grown up in Paris, spoke mainly French and was the butt of jokes by the other girls. Mary Shillito was much depressed also by being separated for the first time from her slightly older sister, whom she considered a goddess. Violet had been sent to Miss Ely's School on Riverside Drive in order to prevent the sisters from speaking French together. Mary thrilled Mabel by her descriptions of the marvelous Violet and her knowledge of the art and music worlds of Paris. "Elle a une telle force d'ame," Mary said of Violet, so feelingly that Mabel longed to know this paragon and to visit Paris.

That this highly sophisticated girl found only Mabel, among all the other girls, responsive to her teaching and sympathetic to her loneliness does forecast the role which Mabel was to play in later life: open to new ideas, fearless of being different, and with a warm interest in others, Mabel attracted numerous important visitors to each home she occupied through her adult life.

By the time June 1896 came, Mabel had persuaded her mother to take her to Paris, where she finally met Mary's sister "Veeolette" and, as promised, immediately sensed "her genius and singular power." Violet had taught herself Italian in order to read Dante, and Greek in order to read Plato in the original. She was studying higher mathematics at the Sorbonne, and could play Beethoven so beautifully that listeners wept. In the weeks when Mabel spent much time with the Shillito sisters in their suite of the family apartment, a whole new world of experiences opened to her. She read their books, went to concerts with them, listened while they talked. It puzzled Mabel that two such ordinary American parents as the Shillitos could have produced such extraordinary daughters. With exquisite taste in dress, at home in Parisian life, they were nevertheless more interested in the inner life. Thus their talk was about the infinite soul, about the works of Balzac or Meliers, about the future of the old social order, about their intuitions concerning life. They walked among the trees of the Bois not to show off new clothes or to pass the time of day with other strollers, but "to feel our souls expand as we . . . talked of our latest observations in the deep sea of the psyche" (254).

Mabel might seem to exaggerate the interest of young girls in the intellectual questions of the day, but no doubt the love which Violet inspired in her was genuine, as their intimacy grew during the summer at Pierrefonds and at the Wagner festival at Bayreuth.

Mabel's last year of school at the Chevy Chase boarding school for girls near Washington, D.C., seems to have been pretty much like all the others—she learned some French, some music, and some skill in character analysis. Then she was finished with formal schooling, was courted during the summer of 1897 by several older suitors of the neighborhood, and like the other girls of wealthy Buffalo families had her coming-out party at the nearby Twentieth Century Club.

Unlike anyone else, however, she had the ballroom decorated like a medieval baronial hall, with great portraits in imitation of Rembrandt and Velasquez on the walls, banners and coats of arms and garlands of holly hanging from the beams, and a wassail bowl carried by two pages dressed for the occasion. Her mother had insisted that their dresses be made in Paris. Mabel recalls, "My dress was of the ultimate French chic, white satin with a small waist, and billowing folds of white net covered all over with hyacinth petals and dewdrops." Nearly everyone invited had sent flowers, so that "several hundred dozens of roses, mostly pink and white, and pounds and pounds of violets were banked up behind us where we stood at the top of the stairs that led down to the Baronial Hall." Mabel, perhaps because of inability to choose among the numerous requests, refused to dance at all. Boredom overcame her as the crowd became more and more disheveled, the room hot and uncomfortable, and her father more and more disgruntled. Toward morning, hardly able to keep her eyes open, her face "stiffened from smiling," she heard her father furiously shout to the musicians, who quickly struck up "Home, Sweet Home," and the guests departed.

It was after five o'clock when the Ganson family climbed the stairs of their own home. "Well, that's over with," exclaimed Mrs. Ganson. Mr. Ganson had already disappeared into his room. Mabel climbed one more flight to her own, as the three ships above the face of the grandfather clock on the landing rocked madly back and forth on the angry sea. And so ends *Background,* the first volume of Mabel's *Intimate Memories.*

Reaction

As one might predict, the reaction of Buffalo socialites to the book when it was published in 1933 was not favorable. Mabel had already become known for the revelations of her relationship to D. H. Lawrence in *Lorenzo in Taos* (1932), but *Background* (1933) exposed living people and a whole social strata to censure. As in any autobiography, it is possible to question the accuracy of a writer in evaluating her own life. In this case, however, Mabel's keen eye for social details and for psychological insights outweigh what her displeased mother and other Buffalo residents considered serious distortions. To most readers the portrayal of a wealthy urban family at the turn of the century rang with truth.

Critics too praised the work. Acknowledging Mabel as a remarkable woman, one critic wrote, "This first volume of her memoirs, which pictures so unforgettably a whole era and a whole society, proves that she is a born writer as well."[2] A London critic noted that "she sketches the portraits of her relatives and friends, of all ages, with a clever and lifelike touch."[3] To William Soskin, Mabel, who in her lifetime "had absorbed the lives of hundreds of men and women," had written "an astonishingly candid and powerful book."[4] Critic E. S. Sergeant admired Mabel's "uncanny intuition" in discovering "any vulnerable point in the Buffalo pattern" and *Background* for its "uncompromising and unforgettable portraiture of well-known social and family figures, swimming in a juice as rich and highly colored as that which sustains the characters of a Bronte novel."[5]

Herbert Gorman, believing that Mabel's life had importance for "the cultural growth of this country," considered *Background* "a genuine addition" to the history of manners in America. "It may not have taken courage to write," he added, "but it certainly took intelligence. And it reveals a capacity for remembering that is unusual and a sure sign of the born *litterateur*."[6] Having been often in the news because of her activities, Mabel now became known as a writer, whose future work promised more telling revelations about her relationships with celebrities in other social milieus.

Chapter Two
Florentine Life:
European Experiences

Depature from Buffalo

Since the frontispiece for *Background* is a photograph of Mabel in her elegant, tight-waisted, Parisian coming-out gown, it is appropriate that she end her first volume of memoirs with her debut, continuing the story of her last few years in Buffalo in her second volume, *European Experiences*. Before starting on this larger canvas, she relates with her usual candor the story of how she happened to become engaged to the son of a neighboring Buffalo family, Karl Evans. Karl was the happy-go-lucky youngest child of the family, who spent most of his days in pleasure boating in the harbor instead of learning the shipping business of his father's Anchor Line. Hunting all kinds of game was also his joy, and a large collection of guns almost his only possession.

Mabel, fun-loving and something of a daredevil herself, was attracted to Karl, who had a slender, graceful body, a bounding step, and a boyish face that often broke into a smile or hearty laugh. Like Mabel, he loved horses and riding and often took part in a polo match at the country club. Mabel had been taught to train green horses for jumping and racing by an older handsome polo player, Seward Cary, who knew no fear and who was so romantic a figure to the young Mabel that, for the sake of his admiration, she faced the danger again and again of being thrown by a rebellious animal. Mabel thus became a match for the daring Karl Evans.

With Karl, she writes, "I lived into the fun of outdoor life, horses and dogs and motorboats." He had also been out in what was then called the Indian Territory and had lived with Indians for months at a time. When he would dress up in a white buckskin chief's dress with a war bonnet and shirt and leggings with long fringes decorated with elk teeth, he looked to Mabel like a "young buck with flashing white teeth." His rust-colored, leathery skin and his untamed Welsh blood made the garb seem fitting. And so Mabel was pleased to "play about with him." She did not consider a serious relationship, however, because she loved reading and quiet contemplation and had "many far thoughts of a life he could never touch" (27).[1]

Karl, however, tricked her into marriage on what she expected to be a mere Sunday outing on the train, supposedly to visit Penjerrick, the Evans's hunting lodge near Youngstown. Instead, Karl and his hunting friend, Jack Piper, enticed Mabel and her friend Charlotte off the trolley car to "visit" a little stone church from which the Sunday parishioners were emerging in order to ride to Youngstown. When the four arrived at the chancel rail of the pretty little church, the minister, in robes, came forward, greeted Karl with the words, "Is this the young lady?" and requested that Mabel and Karl kneel before him. As Mabel turned to flee, she was faced directly by Jack Piper, who had "the most ruthless and determined look I had ever yet had brought to bear on me." She sank upon her shaking knees and was married—although, according to her account, "All my thoughts had been given to not marrying" (33).

Mabel writes of the incident that it "was one of the few things I have ever had done to me in my life." Most things, even if foolish, she had decided for herself or thought she had, but now she was married—"the passive, the truly female experience." Since neither Mabel nor Karl dared tell their parents of their marriage, each continued to live at home while surreptitiously fitting out a tiny house which they managed to furnish through the sale of some of Mabel's jewelry. The front room they decorated with Karl's guns and Indian beadwork and buckskin. When with the help of the family physician they broke the news to her parents, her father took to his bed, and her mother, after some tears, began to plan for a grand, "real" wedding at Trinity Church.

In early October of the first year of the century, Mabel was married by her grandmother's minister, Dr. Davis, by her mother's high church Father Sturgis, and by the bishop of New York State. Dressed in "swathing ivory satin and a cloud of lace," she was escorted down the broad church aisle on the arm of her Grandfather Cook, who, due to the refusal of her father to play the role, had come from New York for the occasion. Six bridesmaids in various shades of pastel and six immaculate ushers, brothers and cousins of Karl, participated in the ceremony before the important people of Buffalo. Mabel "tried to

look dignified and obedient and as though bestowed upon another,"
she says with some suggestion that she played the expected role of
woman being passed from one man to another with some question of
its justice.

As she wrote of the event thirty-five years later from her home in
Taos, she expressed a certain cynicism concerning the celebration and
the crowd in the church "dressed in rich velvet and silk clothes" who
"sparkled slightly with jewels and vibrated with pearls and ivory
smiles." She felt that she and Karl were two strangers who made their
exit through a gathering of strangers. "We were the myths of their
own interpreting temperaments," she says. Perhaps more than she
recognized, she was also the myth that Karl had created. His wedding gift to her had been a silver mounted gun, hers to him a beautiful pair of hunting dogs, and their honeymoon two weeks of deer-
hunting in the Adirondacks at a tiny hunting lodge decorated with
deer heads on the walls and smelling of pancakes and stale tobacco
smoke.

Thus began what was to be a short life together. Little more than
a year passed before Mabel gave birth to a son, and Karl soon after
was fatally shot by a friend who, walking behind him to the duck
blind, had accidentally emptied an entire charge into Karl's back.
Mabel, already weakened by an operation following the birth of her
child and emotionally emptied by the recent death of her father, was
overcome by Karl's violent end. Although Mabel did not know the
friend who had shot him, she insisted, in view of Karl's last words—
"Tell Bris it's all right"—that he be one of the pall-bearers, among
all the Evans relatives. Since he lived in Canada on the other side of
the river, she never saw him afterward, although he did send, by his
weeping young wife, Karl's gold watch, which Mabel later gave to
her son John Evans.

Mabel, in relating this part of her life, is a better narrator of her
own feelings than of the life around her. She fails to mention the important Pan-American Exposition of 1901, with its artificially constructed canals in imitation of Venice and its lake and decorated park,
a festive place for many people of all classes in Buffalo, or the tragic
assassination of President McKinley on 6 September at the exposition. One would think that an autobiographer so much involved in
the city and having lived there since birth would refer to these
events. Since McKinley hovered between life and death until 14 Sep-

tember, the talk of that time and place must have been almost exclusively of the president.

But her mind was on her child. Through her happy pregnancy, which made her lethargic and home-bound by choice, she stitched drawerfuls of clothes and planned for the baby "contented and occupied and unthinking." Surprisingly, when he was born, Mabel did not wish to see the baby who had brought her such pain. She resented her changed state of consciousness, the return of her soul to her body. With the long dreamlike period of gestation over, she now faced the "bitterness of that return to knowledge and feeling and the estimations of the psyche." Thus she returned to "real life"—with great reluctance, after a period in which she was "really detached and invulnerable—all in all to nature."

The baby grew healthily through the next few years, with Mabel and her mother, both widows now, occupying nearby houses. In her intimate recollections, however, Mabel now makes a leap of several years: "a year or two after . . . I was about twenty-two . . . I had a nervous breakdown and my mother sent us to Europe for a change." Mabel must have been considerably older than twenty-two, and her setting out for Europe with two nurses and child, "sadly and without interest," must rouse the reader's suspicion that she is not revealing all the truth. Perhaps Emily Hahn is right that Mabel's love affair with the family doctor forced Mrs. Ganson to remove this troublesome daughter from Buffalo, a city to which the younger woman never returned to live.[2]

Given the nature of Mabel Ganson Evans, it is not surprising that on the ship to France, dressed in her best white China silk gown, she was noticed by the young man across the table, architect Edwin Dodge. A resident of Boston, he was on his way to Paris for a two-month vacation. Although she was met at the dock by her old friend Mary Shillito, and Mr. Shillito, both in deep mourning for the death of Violet and Mrs. Shillito, her days in Paris became occupied with the man in whose profession she had at least an extremely active amateur's interest, and with whom she could converse in almost professional terms. Mabel describes her chagrin, after breaking an engagement with the Shillitos "because of illness" in order to have dinner with Edwin, in discovering her old friends at the same restaurant. When Mary called on Mabel the next morning in the room bedecked with flowers for her "sick" friend, she could not help crying, for, having praised Mabel to her father, she now had to accept his opinion of that young woman as "déclassée."

Soon Mabel and Edwin were engaged. Her grandmother Ganson was pleased enough by news of a wedding to travel to Paris herself with her clergyman, Dr. Jessup, to be present for the ceremony which took place on 3 October 1904 in the Parisian church of St. Sulpice. The couple's being married in Paris rather than Buffalo may mean that there had been a scandalous love affair—from which Mabel had not entirely recovered—for she seems to have felt unrelated to her new husband for many months. At the ceremony her young son, just as the vows were being exchanged, had cried out, "I don't want to be married!" perhaps expressing some of Mabel's own feeling.

Still in an unhappy state after some weeks on the Riviera, Mabel received a visit from Mrs. Ganson, who seemed very unlike the woman Mabel had known as a child. The cold, staid mother and wife, who had never caressed her child nor spoken other than belligerently to her husband, now "blooming in light silk dresses," appeared to be all out "for ease and enjoyment." Also, Mabel remembers, she was "delighted to see John and me . . . settled in a nice house with . . . an amusing young husband." In view of the stony face that Mabel had assigned to her mother previously, it is almost incredible that she now writes of "her sallies of flushed laughter" and her "attempts to be funny." Although Edwin good-naturedly ministered to Mrs. Ganson and other guests, Mabel, with "singular dog-in-the-manger behavior," neither wanted Edwin's attentions nor wanted to share them.

Up at the Villa Curonia

Mabel gradually recovered her spirits through a series of moves that made her mistress of the Villa Curonia in Florence and one of the best-known hostesses in all Europe for almost a decade. Mabel describes her first evening in Florence: as she leaned from the window of the great hotel on the Arno, she says, "The strange odor of Florence mounted to me . . . damp, old stone . . . the odor of dust and roses, . . . delicious to my senses, but not a part of me." With her usual determination, she speaks to "the indifferent old city" in words of challenge: "I will make you mine" (95). There is little doubt that with the help of her architect husband, who saw to much of the restoration of the old villa which they bought, she did just that.

Perhaps, indeed, part of Mabel's perversity during the honeymoon months was the result of physical difficulties resulting from the birth of her large baby, which an operation in Buffalo did not correct. In any case she submitted to an operation in Florence, almost dying from postoperative bleeding. If we can believe Mabel's story, the attending nurse whispered without tact during the crisis, "Oh, my dear, I thought you were gone," and she heard the doctor try to comfort Edwin with "Mon pauvre monsieur." But she recovered by drawing slow deliberate breaths with a minimum of effort and conservation of oxygen. As often, a voyage so near the other world changed her view of life, restoring her emotional health, removing her jealousy of Edwin, and endowing her with the confidence to make not only Florence, but later New York City as well, her own.

Almost immediately in Florence Mabel began to get acquainted, as she did everywhere, with the misfits as well as the prominent. In spite of complaining, *"People*! Never for fifty years, have I left off pursuing, fusing, speculating, identifying, grouping, devouring, and rejecting! . . . Life is in the natural world," she collected natives and visitors to Florence almost as she collected valuable artifacts for the Villa Curonia to decorate its every room.

One of the most interesting of the visitors was Pen Browning, the son of Robert and Elizabeth Barrett Browning, whom Mabel describes as "a small red apple of a man with a plump little figure" (115). His "round red, bald head and smooth, red cheeks" added to his fat figure, seem to make Mabel's designation apt. Unprepossessing as he may have been, with his tiny tooth-brush-like mustache and his "unusually webby" eyelids, which looked Mongolian, Mabel was extremely fond of him. He visited often at the Villa Curonia, and the Dodges went to stay with him in Asolo, where he lived in the very house in which Pippa, of Browning's poem, had lived. Pen, a sculptor, had suffered, in Mabel's opinion, from the evil lies about him spread through Europe by his estranged wife.

When the Dodges visited Asolo, Mabel saw the sculpted figure of Ginerva, the "splendid-looking blond Italian" who had been the only one to successfully nurse the sick, neurotic Mrs. Pen. In the pose, Ginerva is a surprised Eve on her knees, holding an apple with a single bite taken from it; a huge serpent with head raised is beside her, poised to strike. Mabel, who saw great artistry in the piece, believed it could have given rise to the scandal of Ginerva as Pen's mistress (although the woman was happily married to an Italian in the valley) and to the ludicrous story of snakes as inhabitants of his basement. Mabel describes the house at Asolo as fitting for Pen, who had a large number of "brown dachshunds, soft and shiny as silk," as well as light blue and yellow macaws on perches in the garden. Pen was to her always something of a little boy, not imaginative, but good-natured, who always looked puzzled when he heard scandal character-izing him as that terrible man—for, says Mabel, he had nothing of "terribleness" about him.

What Mabel most admired about Pen, however, was his devotion to an unfortunate Florentine, Bindo Peruzzi di Medici. This unfor-tunate marchese, the last of the Medici, was the son of an Italian fa-ther and an American mother, Marchesa Edith Peruzzi, who tried to protect him through a series of scandals which caused his resignation from the army and his retreat to an apartment in her palazzo in Flor-ence. When young, Pen Browning had been in love with the Mar-chesa, and in middle age continued to be one of the few to visit and befriend her handsome son. Mabel writes that "Pen was loyal right to the end, adding thereby to the burden of opprobrium he had so fatally accumulated upon himself," for none of the established fami-lies of Florence would visit Bindo or even speak to him on the street (115).

As for Mabel, she loved and admired both these men. Even though she enjoyed being acquainted with prominent families in Florence, who visited the Villa Curonia and whose houses she and Edwin vis-ited, she was not swayed by fear of losing her reputation. A very close friendship grew up, therefore, between her and Bindo, who had few friends of his own. As they sat by the fire in the twilighted high room over tea, he grew intimate, and she gave "friendship, sympa-thy, understanding" to the young man who was "so dear, so appeal-ing, so magnetic in some unnatural way."

Edwin, however, who was not fond of Bindo, gave Mabel the choice of visiting America or permanently remaining alone in Flor-ence. Writing a note to Bindo, which, as is the case with romantic love notes throughout history, was not delivered, Mabel sadly crossed the ocean with her husband, and upon their return failed to greet Bindo in passing on the street one day. That same night, in the Pa-lazzo, the young man shot himself. Mabel writes, somewhat melo-dramatically, "Ever since then, for Bindo's sake, . . . I have been a friend to those . . . driven by some fatality, . . . from the path over which they were intended to pass" (130). Although Mabel was not one to show a bleeding heart toward humanity as a whole, for homosexuals and others who lived partially outside the acceptable social codes she felt great sympathy. She suffered from Edwin's remark upon hearing of Bindo's death—"And a good thing, too"—and from her own inability to provide Bindo with needed friendship.

Mabel describes the renovating and decorating of the Villa Curonia with architectural discernment. Besides such physical details as the size of the rooms, the shape of the windows, the direction they faced, the nature of the light that entered summer or winter, the material of the floors and paneling, the height of the ceilings, and the colors and shapes of drapes and furniture, she also conveys the emotional response that each part of the Villa evoked in her. Set in the hills above Florence, it was a steep climb for their turn-of-the-century Renault on a road that proceeded slantwise up one side of the mountain and then took a sharp turn to make it to the top of the rising slope on which the villa stood. Looking down toward Florence from this height, they could see the church of San Miniato atop a lower hill and down in Florence the round dome of the cathedral of Florence with Giotto's tower dimly outlined against it.

They also looked down more immediately below them on what was formerly the royal villa of archdukes, now a school for girls. The town itself "lay far below in a huddle of pale opal colors," while opposite, across Florence, they viewed that "tumbled heap of solid shapes," the Apennine Mountains. Always Mabel seemed to want to contrast man and nature. Whereas her life in Florence consisted of talk of great art and artists, of Dante, Michelangelo, and Giotto, of newer artists and architects, of treasures exhibited in some museum, the mountains remained aloof and "brooded over the scene below." Their tallest peak, Monte Morello, forecast the weather: if it was clouded the Florentines expected rain. Man's hurried daily occupations in this fascinating city of art and history thus weighed light in contrast to the unmoving majesty of the natural towers of stone above them.

Although Edwin was in charge of the architectural reconstruction of the Villa Curonia, which had been named for the Russian province of Kurland, home of the former owners, Mabel was as delighted as he at the discoveries they made in adding to and repairing the old building. The main entrance consisted of two huge double doors that opened upon a small high-walled courtyard, through which one had to pass to enter the large reception hall of the house, giving a visitor dismal expectations of the whole. Edwin and Mabel were delighted, therefore, to discover, not buried pearls or vases as in some old villas, but a beautiful courtyard with large stone columns topped by Corinthian capitals, which had been walled in by ugly brick and plaster. Through removal of this added stonework, a magnificent entrance into a perfect fifteenth-century courtyard of magnificent proportions was revealed. Mabel herself, "trailing long silks and chiffon veils," felt quite grand as she descended from her car—which after the steep climb and the wide sweeping curve had come to a stop at the heavy doors—and pushed open the doors with her weight before the servants could assist her. To add to the grandeur of the court she and Edwin placed high on the pillars long silk Sienese banners, which waved gently when anyone entered the enclosure.

Mabel delights in long descriptions of the various salons, the bedrooms and halls, the dining room and courtyards, and terraces and balconies. We read with some amusement, however, "The kitchen was one of the most attractive rooms in the house, but I only remember ever going out to it but once." Obviously a plethora of servants kept the villa running without aid from its mistress. Mabel amiably describes an intricately carved door frame which she and Edwin placed against one wall of the North Salon, across which they hung a fine embroidered curtain. Mabel calls the frame "a very fair symbol of myself at that time, for it led nowhere." As Mabel analyzes her Florentine life it seems to her that she had sunk into the depths of her great Italian bed with its four huge gilded lions' heads guarding her from every direction and has lost touch with the outside world, as she gazed at the blue bedroom walls, "dappled, shimmering, pale" and covered with romantic medieval tapestries. With the smell of jasmine and the songs of the workers in the olive fields below pouring through the embroidered curtains, she was lulled by dreams in this palace where to pass from bedroom to the little yellow salon next door, was hardly to do more than to pass from blue and gold to yellow, and from bed to chaise lounge. A log fire heated the jonquil-yellow room in winter, throwing light on the shelves of books and bibelots and on her large collection of modeled dogs of all sizes and breeds, which stood on shelves, on the chimney piece, on tables, on commodes, dogs standing, sleeping, sitting, pointing. In this small salon Mabel entertained guests for after-dinner coffee and conversation, and here she sat after breakfast in bed surrounded by her "fantastic, feminine oddments" (162).

Creating the Villa Curonia was "a career in itself." In spite of the little sympathetic love she seems to have had for Edwin, Mabel did experience pleasure in working with him to bring a unique villa into existence. In his bedroom on the floor above hers was a trapdoor through which he could descend on a silken ladder into hers, a trip she did not encourage him to make often, for he looked Bostonian rather than romantic on the ladder as "his coat rode up between his shoulder-blades" while he groped for the next rung, unable to make the haste for which such a ladder was designed (159).

In spite of her pleasure in the house, she dreamed of a more romantic role than that of wife and mistress of the villa: "As I walked through the rooms, over and over again I felt I was made for noble love, not for art, not for work, not for the life of the wordly world, but for the fire of love in the body, for the great furnace of love in the flesh, lighted in the eyes and flowing, volatile, between the poles" (197). It is a comment like this perhaps that causes a male critic to label her merely "another rich and restless woman," and causes a modern female critic to see a "self-image that insists on the self as powerless and dependent, while concealing the energy of anger."[3] Mabel's compelling interest in the art of Florence and in the magnificent works of the Renaissance sculptors and painters made her dissatisfied with the men she knew in the flesh. The marble males had *"bodies"* and stood nobly. "One could read their gestures, their poses, their expressions, as though one read a rich and varied language." Nowhere could she find a living "David," like either Michelangelo's or Donatello's.

Like the mousy, well-behaved mate to her proud peacock, which stayed away for three days in spite of the squaking protests of the male but returned bedraggled to follow him as usual, Mabel engaged in a few amours, but always returned to the propriety of her marriage to Edwin. "For," she writes, "it was impossible not to respond to his even-tempered generous nature and his gayety." Her main complaint was that he seemed uninterested in the "deeper undercurrents" of life, experiencing to her mind only the surface and never attempting to analyze his world, whereas she was frequently concerned with her inner life and needs.

Paradoxically, although she complained at times that there were always too many guests at the Villa, that she could never be alone, she nevertheless encouraged their coming and was never happier, it would seem, than when analyzing them. The books published in the mid-1930s made use of notes and letters that she had written at or near the time of the events described. No matter how much she might complain of having no time to herself, the truth was that she would have been lost without the numerous acquaintances to provide subject matter for her pen and speculation for her mind. Chatting easily with the reader about the various inhabitants of Florence, she sets this one and that one in a frame of her own portraiture. Her keen sense of characterization enables her as well to create a revealing self-portrait. That is, she tries to be honest in taking blame for her un-happy marriage with the "long suffering and always so kind" Edwin Dodge, and in admitting that her own prejudices color her portraitures.

What one wonders most about in the story of the Florentine years, which extended from approximately 1904 to 1912, is the lack of mention of her growing child. The years between three and twelve would seem to have held many memorable events that a mother would have recorded about her only child. Even the return of the family to America for her son's schooling in 1912 seemed more dic-tated by Mabel's desire for a new life than by concern for John's education.

Not so with his tutors, in whom, both male and female, Mabel took great interest. Marguerite Michel, whom Mabel "inherited" from the former owner, the Baroness de Nolde, was "a tall, flat-breasted girl of thirty-eight to forty . . . [with] dark, suspicious eyes that glanced quickly right and left, and a mouth that, when she smiled made her face look strangely wolfish" (277). Having been madly in love with the baroness, she quickly transferred her affection to Mabel, who at first found this "constant vital stream of love" en-trancing. Since jealousy was almost as strong an emotion as love in this humorless woman, however, she expressed the "blackest hate and contempt" for Mabel's guests, mainly ignoring Edwin as an inevita-ble adjunct to the villa. In the end, she did so poison the air, and eventually herself, that she had to be sent to a nursing home in Flor-ence. How John fared with this character, Mabel never relates. In a painting by Jacques Emile Blanche, a turbaned Mabel, dressed in rich flowing Florentine robes, with her feet upon an embroidered cushion, looks wistfully toward the painter, and toys with a long string of beads, while her son of some ten years kneels on the tiger skin rug partially behind her. In a photograph of almost the same pose, al-though Mabel momentarily looks down at the boy and he up at her,

John becomes, as in the portrait, almost part of the background to the costumed woman.

However little importance Marguerite Michel had in the education of the boy, she had considerable in the future life of the villa after her departure. At least according to Mabel's account, she haunted the place for years after her death in the nursing home. Her first victim was a house guest named Maud, a British author of a book on Botticelli, who was awakened by a cold foot which kept pushing her out of the bed in Marguerite's old room. Janet Scudder, an American sculptor whom Edwin had known in Paris, fared so badly in the room that she could not sleep at all, became more and more depressed, and one night took the train for Paris, vowing never to return to that haunted Villa.

It was to Constance Fletcher that the ghostly voice of Marguerite manifested itself. Mabel saw Constance as a pitiful figure, living on dreams of her love for Byron's grandson, Lord Lovelace, who before his desertion had given her his grandfather's miniature and a packet of his letters. Although publishers, collectors, and scholars had visited Venice, Constance hung on to the letters, in spite of her poverty, as sacrosanct evidence of her romance. A successful playwright for a period in London, she had been a friend of Oscar Wilde and of Henry James, who fictionalized her story in *The Aspern Papers* (1888). Constance, on her visits to the Villa Curonia, had been friendly with the austere Marguerite, whose ghost appeared in a lovely glow of light with a sweet voice "like exquisite music" saying, "Yes, it is I. But do not call Mabella." With a beating heart, Constance related the incident to her hostess, who was astonished that this vision had used the pet name which no one else had known.

It was a Swami, however, who finally laid the ghost to rest. Having stuffed all the cracks, he filled Marguerite's room with "a great, sweet, thick cloud" of incense, explaining that the spirits of the dead cannot stand sweet odors, this being the reason we surround the dead with flowers.

After Marguerite, Mabel employed an American male tutor, Paul, but as is usual with Mabel's commentary, we are not told what he taught, only that he was handsome, young, and a good tennis player. He accompanied her on various expeditions with other adult friends to places near Florence and to the Lido in Venice, often when Edwin was away working on architectural projects in America; where John was at times like these, one can only speculate. Mabel does admit to recognizing finally that John at a young age was indeed "lonesome in his rooms." She ruefully admits, "I know it now, but never thought of it in those days." Once when she found him hiding in the middle of her great bed, she quickly bundled him back to his own, in spite of his large, troubled eyes upon her. Fortunately Edwin seems to have been a thoughtful father to the boy. Mabel no doubt cared, but still brought up the boy as she had been brought up, by hired nurses and tutors.

As for the tutor, Mabel recalls his coming to her room one night when Gertrude Stein was a guest. "My natural desire for him was so strong that it passed over me in deep waves like light shaking out of clouds—yet I only clung to him . . . while Gertrude wrote on the other side of the wall, sitting in candlelight like a great Sibyl dim against the red and gold damask that hung loosely on the walls" (332). Perhaps Mabel had read Stendhal's *The Red and the Black,* or perhaps she assumed that the purpose of a handsome tutor was to oblige the mistress of the house. In any case, she virtuously sent the young man back to his own room, not, however, with any thoughts of her only child, whose tutor she was appropriating: her own emotions, not her son's, engaged her.

Leo and Gertrude Stein and Alice B. Toklas

As a collector of celebrities, Mabel gave her attention to many interesting personalities at the Villa Curonia. Among these were Gertrude Stein, whose little essay on Mabel Dodge brought wide acclaim to them both.

Mabel visited the brother and sister, Leo and Gertrude Stein, in Paris at their home, 27 Rue de Fleurus, in 1905, and was much taken with Leo's talk of the new painters, the so-called "Independents," Matisse, Picasso, and Cezanne. So persistent was he in showing off his pictures with the "obstinate look on his face [of an] old ram," that people came to hear his fulminations against any art which "was merely the running of water down-hill." They stayed to listen to his interpretation of the artists he admired, Picasso in particular, who "carried the faculty of seeing farther than natural sight usually allowed" (322). To Leo must be given credit for the gift of seeing farther than those who laughed at the pictures and made fun of him. He stood night after night, Mabel remembers, "wrestling with the inertia of his guests. . . . Always the enemy of gravitation, always the advocate of tension in art." Although Mabel thus gives Leo more credit than Gertrude for sponsoring a new kind of art, she admits that Gertrude, presiding in a large rather bare room against the picture-covered walls, by her very presence exerted an influence upon the future of art and artists.

So much has been written about Gertrude Stein in recent decades that Mabel's words might seem repetitious, but her observations of the now famous writer have a vividness that may well have contributed to many another biographers's account:

Gertrude Stein was prodigious. Pounds and pounds and pounds piled up on her skeleton—not the billowing kind, but massive, heavy fat. She wore some covering of corduroy or velvet and her crinkly hair was brushed back and twisted up high behind her jolly, intelligent face. She intellectualized her fat, and her body seemed to be the large machine that her large nature required to carry it. (324)

Mabel gave Leo credit for the theory of aesthetics that only what pleases the individual is worth consideration, and she perceived Gertrude as his principal disciple and practitioner of the theory. In an era of snobbism in art, Gertrude cared nothing for what others thought was good, and so, pleasing only herself, she eventually pleased the world. Practicing the "same unconventionality" with which the post-impressionists piled cubes on cubes, Gertrude wrote her portrait of Picasso: "This one was one being one having something being coming out of him. This one was one going on having something come out of him."[4] Leo and Gertrude, whose work she much admired, both gave Mabel encouragement to pursue her path with the guidance of her own intuition. Besides furnishing models for two of the skillful portraits which Mabel painted in *European Experiences,* they perhaps helped free her to write adroitly of many others in her autobiographical volumes.

Mabel characterizes Alice Toklas as a dainty catlike woman, who ate sparingly while Gertrude heartily consumed great slices of roast beef. Alice "looked like Leah, out of the Old Testament, in her half-Oriental get-up" (325), with her ear lobes weighted down with long heavy earrings and her straight body covered with batik Japanese prints. Alice loved her hands and used to manicure her fine almond-shaped nails for an hour each morning. Otherwise she gave her time to Gertrude like a handmaiden, making herself indispensable, and ousting Leo, who friendlessly left the Stein establishment for a life in Florence.

From his house in Fiesole, across town, he would wander to Mabel's villa with dusty feet and linger for hours pouring his "puzzling intellectual profundities" in her ear. Mabel noticed that as Gertrude's language became simpler, Leo's became more difficult and ponderous. Working on a jigsaw puzzle, he exclaimed as he slipped in a piece, "I think this angle is susceptible to a conjunction." Mabel, considering that he was grieving for his sister, who, he felt, had been subjugated by a lesser individual, gave him a sympathetic hearing in spite of thinking that his "intricate, webby thought systems" made very little sense. Since Mabel, like Leo, had the greatest admiration and love for Gertrude and very little for Alice, she well understood his need of the companionship which she provided.

The relationship between Mabel and Gertrude remained warm, however, until one occasion when the two visitors from Paris were staying at the Villa Curonia and Alice became exceedingly piqued at the looks which passed between Gertrude and Mabel.[5] From this time on, Mabel felt that Alice tried to separate the two, so that, although no open rift occurred until after Mabel's move to New York City in 1913, it was permanent when the break came. Before that, however, Gertrude, while visiting Mabel during the fall of 1912, wrote the "Portrait" of her hostess. Gertrude's method was to sit at night in her room after everyone was asleep and write automatically "in a long weak handwriting—four or five lines to a page—letting it ooze up from deep down inside her." Then Alice would gather up the sheets in the morning for typing and they would both be surprised and pleased at what Gertrude had written so unconsciously the night before. It turned out that in this case, Mabel too was delighted with what she thought was an honest portrayal, even though to many readers the symbolism was obscure, the syntax hopeless, and the view of Mabel, insofar as anyone could make it out, inaccurate. Undaunted by criticism, Mabel had "Mabel Dodge at the Villa Curonia" printed and bound in Florentine wallpaper, and circulated copies widely among her friends in Florence and New York.

The first sentence—"The days are wonderful and the nights are wonderful and the life is pleasant"—is perhaps the only one in the whole piece in which the syntax and the structure fit traditional expectations. Such a typical short paragraph as the following, however, was incomprehensible to many readers: "Abandon a garden and the

house is bigger. This is not smiling. This is comfortable. There is
the comforting of predilection. An open object is establishing the loss
that there was when the vase was not inside the place. It was not
wandering."[6] Another long sentence picked at random seems to have
no relationship to what precedes and follows, and very little internal
structure. "Not to be wrapped and then to forget undertaking, the
credit and then the resting of that interval, the pressing of the sound-
ing when there is no trinket is not altering, there can be pleasing
classing clothing." Mabel advised that only by feeling the "Portrait"
could one get pleasure from it. It brought many a happy laugh from
her friends as they read it aloud, but everybody had laughed at Picasso too, when Leo showed off his paintings in Paris. Mabel's publicizing Gertrude's sketch finally helped the artist to get a serious
hearing.

Mystifying as the whole thing was to many, Mabel, in November
1912, wrote "Dearest Gertrude" in Paris: "I consider the 'Portrait' to
be a master-piece of success, producing about the same effects as myself were the truth always said!" Although she could quote many lines
of it, she admitted that on some days she did not understand it, but
neither did she understand herself. Another thing for which she
thanked Gertrude was that henceforth her letters came addressed not
to Mrs. Edwin Dodge, wife of the well-known Boston architect, but
to Mabel Dodge herself.[7]

Artistic Visitors at the Villa

If Mabel's account of life at the Villa Curonia and of the visitors
she entertained were nothing but a mundane day-by-day review of
events, the book would have little interest today. Although other
hostesses also lionized famous artistic figures of the first decade of the
century, Mabel could recount her memories in unique language with
an unusual honesty about herself and her subjects.

When she writes of the world's most important stage designer and
theoretician of the times, Gordon Craig, she brings to life his character. When this eccentric genius passed through the narrow streets
of Florence, he looked to her something like Mother Goose, with his
"fine brown hair waving under a low broad-brimmed hat" and his
"long cape flapping in the wind" (347). Although he had annoyed
neighbors by walking naked in his garden, Mabel had invited him to
her villa, where he talked always "of light, of space, and the need for

a new world," which he hoped his massive uncluttered theater staging might help to bring about. Together they inflamed each other's
imaginations through plans for a great pageant reviving the life and
beauty of fifteenth-century Florence and making people ashamed of
"the ugliness of industrialism." Although Mabel lost interest, she
speculated many years later: "After all—Craig and I—if we had put
our forces together?"[8]

In the roles she played in the lives of various important characters
of her times, Mabel might seem to star by virtue of being her own
narrator, but her pictures of many of the greats have a ring of truth,
whether her part in their lives is exaggerated or not. Such is the case
with the great Italian actress, Eleanora Duse. Mabel, on being informed that Duse was pining away in a dark Florentine retreat, invited her to stay at the Villa Curonia, where she could enjoy the open
air in the privacy of the second-story loggia. Mabel describes their
first meeting at the home of Duse:

my heart beat very hard as I waited a moment in an austere, conventional
salon. . . .
    Then Duse flowed up to me; very grave and unsmiling she stood there,
and her eyes were level with mine as she looked from under her triangular-
shaped lids with her head hung back and her chin thrust out. She looked
quite deeply into my eyes, portentous, and took my two hands. She made
a *thing* of it, significant and fateful. I became a trifle cold inside, but I
showed warmth. It was like a slow dance where every moment counts, so
after an interval of silence and exchange, came the beat for speech and she
said, in French, very seriously:
    ". . . I fear I will give you great trouble. . . ."
    "I am only too glad to be of use, Madame," I replied, cold and stately
too. (364)

Duse proved to be the cause of some trouble. Arriving with a
young woman companion in mannish clothes, she occupied Mabel's
great bedroom on the upper loggia, praising its blue damask hangings but disliking that Edwin's bath and bedroom were next door.
Mabel concluded finally that a genius like Duse, whose "consuming
spirit" evinced the ultimate in perception and sensitivity, could be
understood only by a like genius. Although she felt herself to have
superior powers in relating to others, she could not feel any warmth
for Duse's "intoxicating romanticism rising from her gestures and her

voice, from the lines of her clothes, which always fell into noble silhouettes."

If the relationship between Mabel and Duse was cool, however, such was not the case with the *jeune personne,* Signorina R, who immediately began to pursue Mabel and to quarrel all night with Duse, much to Edwin's sleepless disapproval. Mabel is frank to admit her attraction for (and perhaps in some cases, attraction to) other women. One such was the supposed governess, Marguerite Michel; another was the Egyptian Princess Mediha, with whom once, in a Paris hotel, she "wrestled around our salon, knocking over tables and chairs, neither giving in, both delighting in physical power and exercise." Another was Maud, one of a group of English women who lived in Florence without men, who had one of those "things" about Mabel which she used to reveal in overblown compliments on Mabel's dress and beauty. As has been mentioned, Mabel, according to her own account, aroused the antipathy of Alice Toklas because of Gertrude Stein's fond attention.

Among less well known guests whom Mabel entertained at the Villa Curonia were Paul Draper, the brother of the famous actress-monologist Ruth Draper, and his wife. Not the great artist that Ruth Draper was—in a recent biography *she* is said by British actor, John Gielgud, to have been (along with Martha Graham) "the greatest individual performer that America has given us"[9]—Paul Draper was nevertheless a recognized concert tenor. He had come to Florence from New York to study with Isidor Braggiotti and was kept afloat in Florence and in London by his wife Muriel, who entertained after his concerts, curbed his drinking and gambling, accompanied him on the piano, and coached him in the singing of Schumann Lieder, for which he became very well known.

He had to have an extramarital "grand passion" in his life partly because, according to Mabel, it was the convention of the period among musicians. Also at hand was Mabel herself, who admits: "I tried to attract his attention for it was a compulsion with me in those days." Paul Draper thus fell into "the magical hollow dream I used to create around people, and in which they drew delighted breath for a little while" (258). It may be such an evaluation of herself which caused a critic of *European Experiences* to remark of Mabel, "It is the daring, the effrontery, of these 'Intimate Memories' of Mabel Dodge Luhan which constitutes their chief appeal. As in the earlier volume,

'Background,' we are amazed continually at the complete lack of self-consciousness with which she writes."[10]

Robert de la Condamine, "a strange, wonderful fellow," fills only a few pages of Mabel's account of her Florentine years, but lines from his poetic prose piece, "The Upper Garden," furnish a short prefatory quotation for nineteen of her twenty-two chapters. Any application of these headings to the content of the chapters is vague, or perhaps understood only by Mabel herself. For example, her chapter on their renovations of the Villa Curonia is preceded by a quotation from "The Upper Garden": "For as in creation all the emotions are merged into this use of them, and joy and sorrow are here but the shadows of silver, so is the artist concerned but with the shadow of these . . ." (131).

One applicable heading from Condamine—"There are those who leave the world for the garden, and the garden for the Upper Garden, that barren and sweet place"—precedes the chapter "Marcelle," concerning the religious friend who tried to convert Mabel to Catholicism. Condamine lived in an old exotic apartment, its walls lined with greenish mirrors "that seemed to turn it into a deep-sea neighborhood." When he presented her with a copy of "The Upper Garden," he inscribed it: "To Mabel Dodge, who has the courage to sit still and the wisdom to keep silent" (267). Perhaps this succinct description has more accuracy and judgment than anything in his book, for her ability to provide an atmosphere in which others could converse seems to have attracted the prominent and the interesting to her homes, wherever she lived.

To the Villa Curonia besides writers, designers, dancers, actresses, singers, and sculptors, came painters, one of whom, Jacques Emile Blanche—portraiturist of such French artists as Monet, Manet, and Degas, and of such British writers as George Moore, Thomas Hardy, and Henry James—did several portraits of Mabel in his Paris studio and later in the Grand Salon of her villa in Florence. Two of these appear as illustrations in *European Experiences,* Mabel looking romantically dreamlike in turban and flowing Florentine gown. Obviously her talk of Picasso or Matisse, at which he always looked "reluctant and alarmed," had no effect on this traditional painter, who "hounded the souls of his sitters" in an attempt to portray their depths. He took liberties in the characterizations of some of his subjects, for example, *Gide et ses amis* shows André Gide with a group of blacks in rich Asiatic dress seated on the floor around him. Mabel saw Blanche as one of those charming men, who, though they do not know it, "owe their ease and grace and aplomb to their wives," for whom Mabel also has a barb, calling them "maternal women who keep society infantile." In her analysis of the sexes, Mabel often evinces anomalous feelings, sometimes seeing the male as a necessary complement to the female, but perhaps more often, as with Blanche, seeing him as somewhat childish and dependent upon a woman, who is nevertheless not free herself because of the role she must play. It would seem however, that Madame Blanche and her spinster sisters, taking interminable imaginary trips by means of the maps which they spread each night upon the table, were more self-sufficient in Mabel's eyes than Blanche, who needed the constant approbation of his wife.

Another artist, the sculptor Jo Davidson, modeled a head in clay of Mabel Dodge when he and his wife visited at the Villa Curonia. As reproduced in *European Experiences,* it shows a rather determined woman with an uncertain smile, her hair in large buns wound over the ears and bangs across the mid-forehead. In his autobiograpy, Davidson writes: "Mabel, dressed in a Venetian gown, floated through the vast halls looking for all the world as if she had always been a part of the *mise en scène.* . . . I did a bust of Mabel Dodge. I would watch for that enigmatic smile of expectancy and wonder, 'What is she plotting now?' "[11] Davidson also testifies to what he calls "the lugubrious playfulness" of some ghostly presence which began to disturb their sleep, causing them to depart hastily one night for Rome. Mabel, who was never herself troubled by spooks, took great delight, both according to her own account and to that of Davidson, in the distress of the others. She attributes the events to the nervousness of her guests, whereas Davidson writes that Mabel continually brought the conversation around to the quasi-supernatural events in the Villa and concludes, "She knew something would happen—it always did, she saw to that."

Mabel saw Davidson as "full of *bonhomie* and a certain intense energy and *volonté*." Under his thick mass of strong, rough black hair and his bushy eyebrows, his dark, brown eyes above his short beard showed through his hairiness on "the best little face in the world, perpetually in motion, twinkling and cheerful" (433), hardly the type to have been frightened by a ghost nor to have taken part in an exorcism conducted by a priest from the monastary in Arcetri. According to Mabel, however, "Jo followed first," as the priest, "in a white lace dress," accompanied by two young Italian boys "also in white

95986

LIBRARY
COLBY-SAWYER COLLEGE
NEW LONDON, N.H. 03257

dresses," paraded through the rooms shaking censers of burning incense. Although Davidson does not mention this ritual he does admit
to sleeping more soundly on the night train to Rome than at the
villa. He also admits being glad to leave behind Mabel's Italian butler, Domenico, who had been "suspiciously solicitous" about the
events of the previous nights.

Of other prominent guests such as Arthur Rubinstein and André
Gide, Mabel makes only passing mention in her published work.
Whether they come in for fuller treatment in her lengthier unpublished accounts can only be known when her papers in the Beinecke
Library at Yale become available in the year 2000. Rubinstein himself, however, has given a description of Mabel, when she was about
thirty, as having "a pleasant face, a slightly too generous figure, and
the fixed, absent smile of a Mona Lisa."[12] He was amazed at her gift
for gathering together the most incongruous of guests, to make life
at the villa resemble a "constant carousel." He, like others, testifies
to the silence of his hostess: "She spoke in monosyllables, except
when addressing the servants, and she answered any query with a
short nod." Since it is difficult to get into an argumentative wrangle
with such a conversationalist, it must have been the guests who provided any sparks of wit or heat, the hostess providing only the setting. When they parted, Rubinstein remembers, Mabel gave
"another of her enigmatic smiles and a significant nod." Evidently
she was no more chatty in parting with her guests than in entertaining them. Rubinstein elaborates on the "carousel" image of the villa.
"There were two shrieking Englishwomen whose names I have forgotten, and, as if it weren't enough, a continuous flow of extraneous
persons were constantly invading the premises from morning until
night. We had Gertrude Stein, engaged in some interminable vocal
battles with Van Vechten, Reed hating everything and everybody,
. . . Whenever or whatever I played, whether Beethoven or Stravinsky, some of those present would leave the room in protest, hating
the one or the other." If Rubinstein could not say much for the company, he did, however, find the Villa Curonia a beautiful place, with
its Renaissance palazzo "surrounded by tall cypresses and fragrant
flower beds" and with its vast loggia which opened "onto the soft
neighboring hills."

In a parody of Mabel's account of her life in Florence, Cornelia Otis
Skinner paints a like picture of the confusion among the guests. She

entitles her piece "A Brief Digest of the Intimate Memoirs of Mabel Fudge Hulan":

> That summer I moved to Florence. Everyone of importance followed me there. They all lived in the villa. Some had to sleep on the stairs or in cinquecento chests. Only to rare souls did we allot the privilege of sleeping in the lovely old well, carved by Benvenuto Cellini. . . . I was . . . glamorous in asphodels and conch shells and an exquisite Etruscan toga my spaniel had dug up near the Farnese cesspool. Sargent painted me in that delicious costume. Later he destroyed the canvas. My smile eluded him.[13]

Besides celebrities, Mabel also from time to time entertained artistic women friends from America. Tante Rose Clarke, who had been her art teacher in Buffalo, lived in one end of the Villa for a long period, keeping innumerable cats in her room and occasionally tutoring John. As the number of cats increased, however, and her pictures remained unfinished, Mabel had to forcibly dislodge this lonely woman, who in the beginning had helped choose the furniture and the decoration for various rooms. New York painter Mary Foote, "plain as a perch" but with a great sense of humor, visited from time to time, bringing her paints and working often on the loggia overlooking Florence. On one occasion Jo Davidson, although he had not painted before, used Mary's paints to make a sketch of Mabel's young son, sitting "with his arms about his bare, drawn-up knees, scowling prodigiously," a picture which Mabel kept as a memory of peaceful days on the loggia. Janet Scudder, a sculptor from Indiana who had a studio in Paris, "was a real person" with "provocative American humor that bites into every disguise." In spite of four marriages and several love affairs, Mabel seems to have had special affinity for a close woman friend with whom to laugh about the foibles of men.

Edwin and the Failure of a Marriage

One might think that the Villa Curonia was Mabel's alone, so little does Edwin figure in it. If her son played a small part in the account of her life in Florence, her husband seems to have played no more. Even in the chapter toward the end of *European Experiences* which is titled "Edwin," he is treated only superficially, much more attention being given to Mabel's descriptions of Italian food and Parisian clothes. Furthermore, the chapter is headed, most inappropriately, by a line from Browning's poem, "Up at a Villa—Down in the City," in which the speaker laments his inability to afford a house on the city square. The Dodges had plenty of money. They were not "beggars" but "choosers" of the Villa Curonia with its beautiful view of the city below. Still it is possible to say of Mabel's growing unhappiness with Edwin, "Ah, the pity, the pity!" Even while admitting his virtues—the book is dedicated "For Edwin, long-suffering and always so kind"—Mabel feels that after eight years she must part from this commonsense American, who, to one reviewer, "stands out as the only sound person in these picaresque revelations of a latter-day Amazon."[14]

Although they had motored all over Italy, visiting the churches and tasting the wine of each area, and had often traveled to Paris for shopping and dining and viewing the crowds at the horse races, Mabel felt that Edwin never shared her imaginative delight in the Italian peasants or in the elegantly dressed Parisians. She recounts little of him except that he once went to Rome to locate her mother's new husband, a retired admiral who had imbibed too many intoxicants.

Thus, as Mabel became more Italianized, the distance widened between the pair, "until the inner separation was pretty complete, made so by my selfish ego, long before I left him" (396). At the end of *European Experiences* she again admits to her failure with Edwin: "I grew more and more unaware of him. He was only the figurehead on my ship" (445). Muriel Draper in an account in *Music at Midnight* likewise seems oblivious of Edwin's presence:

> There was a day in Florence when Mabel Dodge and I had heard of a village for sale. We desired to buy it. It was an old feudal estate, built around a court and comprising every period of architecture that had flourished in Italy from the eleventh century to the late eighteenth. . . . For nearly a hundred years it had been occupied by peasants as a village. It was large enough to house at least three hundred men, women and children, had its own post office, a few shops and possibly a prison or two in a dungeon below ground. We wanted it, we wanted it terribly.[15]

Neither woman apparently thought about consulting Edwin, who, as an architect, would seem to have been at the very least useful in reviewing the building's structure.

As the years went by, moreover, Mabel found that, although she wanted Edwin to "make a part of the background," he fitted this role less well. "He always seemed to laugh at instead of with people, and in the wrong place. He was a wet blanket." Mabel felt that the conversation among her guests was limited by his "inferior sophistication" and "his facetious, Boston humor" (446). In *Ladies Bountiful,* W. G. Rogers describes Mabel as one who, much as she loved to collect physical things, from Buddhist figurines to hoards of bronze, silver, lacquer, and bone dogs, found even more excitement in bountifully providing for the men and women whom she also collected for her pleasure.[16] When Edwin finally failed to fit into her pattern of life, even as part of the background, she determined in 1912 to return to America—with great misgivings and presumably for the sake of her son's schooling, but actually perhaps to escape from a relationship which would never be broken by her ever-patient and loving husband, whose eyes, she writes, "always seemed to be upon me" (445).

Attuned to the life in Florence for nearly a decade, she faced with reluctance the return to New York City, which was nevertheless "the only place to live" if she went back. As she struggled with her own feelings, however, she admits that the romanticism of artistic Florence, which she had imagined peopled with Renaissance figures through the years, was also losing its novelty, and that the vast company of "friends" she had visited and entertained had become boring. She no longer "mooned" along the Ponte Vecchio or visited the Pitti Palace, or strolled along the Arno with pleasure. The people she knew in Florence came to seem like portraits in a picture gallery. It was only her feeling that life in New York "seemed just too dreary and unattractive for words" that made her, on the passage home, sit "at the rear of the ship with my back turned to the bow, facing back, towards Europe, for that, at least, I knew" (452). She expresses what haunts any individual facing a new life after leaving the old.

Critical Reaction

Critics responded to *European Experiences* with grudging praise. Fanny Butcher wrote, "Mabel Dodge Luhan has done literature a service in recording with the enthusiasm of a participant a period and social scene which have all of the charm of the excitedly unimportant."[17] According to Isabel Patterson, when Mabel writes of third-rate people, her style is third rate, but "It conveys what it describes, which most third-rate writing does not." The same critic also admits

that Mabel once in a while "sees something which evokes an authentic note."[18]

M. L. Becker, likewise, reluctantly praises the book: "It may in-
furiate you, it may make you slightly sick in spots, but it will hold
you. You cannot stop reading it. Moreover, it will be for various rea-
sons worth reading."[19] Although Mabel was called "a confirmed romantic," it may actually be the realistic portrayal of herself and
others that made the book "infuriatingly readable" to critic Mina
Curtis and that appealed to the "outraged but absorbed" audience of
the 1930s, when frank autobiographical revelations were less common
than in the 1980s.[20]

Chapter Three
Life and Friends in New York: *Movers and Shakers*

Mabel Dodge aptly gave the third volume of her *Intimate Memories* the title of *Movers and Shakers* (1936).[1] During the years 1912 to 1917, while she lived at 23 Fifth Avenue in New York City, she was attracted to and had an attraction for numerous political activists, artists, journalists, and writers who helped determine the course of American thought before and after World War I.

Entertaining in a large second-floor flat on lower Fifth Avenue, which was decorated mainly in stark white, she made the acquaintance of a variety of New Yorkers, a number of whom wrote about her in their accounts of the time, verifying the reliability of Mabel's own story. In a typical review of the book, Stella J. Roof wrote. "Mrs. Luhan's flair for interesting people has produced a treasure of source-material, both in scope and in documentation. And a joy for the Great Public. For aside from its wealth of savory gossip about celebrities, the book is alive with vivid comedy."[2] Now instead of the Europeans of Mabel's second volume of memoirs, radical and artistic American visitors frequented her fashionable salon in New York.

Hutchins Hapgood

One of Mabel's early and most long-lasting friendships was with the writer Hutchins Hapgood, whose autobiography, *A Victorian in the Modern World* (1939), describes a number of incidents in his life in which Mabel played an important part. Hutch had been born in Chicago a decade before Mabel Ganson was born in Buffalo. A liberal political thinker, he had written for the *Chicago Evening Post* before coming to New York, where after working for several other newspapers be became an editorial writer for the *New York Globe,* producing articles in behalf of free speech, labor unions, and other liberal causes which made him well-known. His semidocumentary of the underworld, *The Autobiography of a Thief* (1903), and his *The Spirit of Labor* (1907), written from interviews with laboring men and women, had the purpose of describing "the underprivileged in their attempt to bend the social forms into shapes which would enable them to live more freely."[3] He wrote a preface to Alexander Berkman's *Prison Memoirs of an Anarchist* (1912), which helped explain the situation that led Berkman to try to shoot steel magnate Henry Frick. In the forefront of those working for social change in the early years of the century, he saw himself as having grown to maturity in the unchanging Victorian age of the horse and buggy, only to be hurled into the twentieth century, with its self-propelled vehicles bringing social problems unthought of in the past. He was not one to sit quietly by without trying to ameliorate some of the social evils which the growth of cities and the fast progression of industrialization were bringing about.

Mabel Dodge was also in some sense a Victorian in the modern world, but she directed her efforts toward self-realization rather than improvement of the social situation. Nevertheless, she and Hutchins Hapgood became the closest of friends, and had many activist friends in common. Hapgood, a writer himself, thought Mabel's *Movers and Shakers* very good. He extends "sincerest praise for the essential literary art disclosed in the book. Many literary critics, including some of the very best, would condemn the book even as a piece of literature on account of the lack of conscious writing and of concentrated attention to details of style," he comments. "But many of the pages of this book vibrate with life; many personages live again; and large sections of that scene and period of time recall to us, who went through them, their characteristic rhythm."[4]

Hapgood himself is one of the personages who lives in the pages of the third volume of Mabel's biography. He was her confidant during the years she lived in New York, relieving what she calls "the perplexity about my marriage to Edwin." Her uprooting from Italy had required vast adjustments in living and new perceptions of reality; cultural changes brought psychological problems, which she weathered with the help of her friend Hutch. "I talked and talked to him," she writes, "trying by the sound of words to understand what was happening to me" (17–18).

Mabel also knew Neith Boyce Hapgood, Hutch's wife who loved Hutch but who disregarded his political ideas, considering them "no more important to real life than a bunch of red and blue balloons."

Neith "moved like a slow river and . . . had sleepy, green eyes that sometimes woke up." The problem was that Hutch could never reach her soul and make himself known to her. Therefore, in spite of what was a happy marriage, Hutch, like Mabel, needed someone to talk to, someone who listened, an art which Mabel cultivated (48). Mabel was no more concerned with Hutch's social views than was Neith, and of the books he wrote she seems to have most admired his *The Story of a Lover* (1919)—a confessional account of his relationship with his wife, which Mabel thought a tour de force. How few people, was her claim, can write so honest a story "about real life in an urge to understand it and to make it understood."

Granting that Mabel had more interest in gathering to herself the prominent reformers than in initiating social change, Hutch nevertheless respected her search for what she and he called "It." Since he had studied philosophy in Germany and had read the great speculative works of the Western world, his pursuit of "the Infinite" was different from hers, but he understood her quest for the Cause of things. Although to Hutch most pretty women attracted men by their appearance of having "roots in the ground and a possibility of eternal flowering," Mabel was rootless "like a cut flower" (349), and hence had to spend her life searching for nourishment wherever she could find it. In various letters through the years, Mabel wrote him that in spite of new friendships, "My spirit reaches out to you." Only Hutch could satisfy the inner need she had for understanding; only he had the "reassuring quality" that brought her comfort. She also gave him credit for the success of her salon on Fifth Avenue "and the particular thing we all created there for a moment." In 1926 she wrote, "After all it was you who really started it there, for *you* first gave me a sense of renewed life."[5]

Tangible evidence of Mabel's lasting regard for Hapgood is her reprinting in *Movers and Shakers* of an eight-line poem called "My Belovèd," which she says she wrote for him and which Emma Goldman published in *Mother Earth* in 1913: As the seeker of the poem passes through the dusky streets to find "my belovèd" among the "dim shapes," she concludes, "In my passing a blind old cripple caught at my heart,/And turning, I found in his eyes my belovèd." (55) The sympathy that Hutch had for the unfortunate of the world seems to have moved Mabel to a like sympathy in this expression of her affection for a man who identified with her own uncertainties about life and about herself.

Edwin Arlington Robinson

Among the greats whom Mabel knew was Edwin Arlington Robinson, one of America's most important poets, whom she refers to as
E. A. Although he may not have been a recluse, still there are not
many women who could claim to have lunched and corresponded
with him as she did. Having met him where he was living in the
Staten Island home of Clarissa Davidge, she took him to lunch a
number of times at Poligniani's, "where the Italian cooking was better than in Italy." Although she preferred to eat at home, which "was
altogether more agreeable than any place one had to go," the need to
expend some energy "sent one catapulting into the street and whizz-
ing away in the motor." Still she must have looked very contented
there, for Robinson chided her, "Surely you don't want to make me
think you're happy" (43). Mabel implies that in his view of the world
as "a kind of spiritual kindergarten where millions of bewildered in-
fants are trying to spell 'God' with the wrong blocks," he saw her as
typical.[6]

According to her account, a rapport existed between them from the
time of their first meeting. Mabel, making a show of "silence and
apathy" in the midst of animation at the luncheon table with the
poet, "caught him straight and won an instant answer—a flicker of
understanding." Even though Mabel considered Robinson a "stingy,
inhibited man," she appreciated this "tiny, shy, burning, and directed glance." In that same brief instant his solemn look was over-
ridden "by a Yankee, twisted smile that spelled hardtack, axes,
gnarled logs," and that showed, "resident within him, a humorous
common sense, deeper than any present woe." So, according to Mabel, the two were "cronies, pals, comrades, friends, affinities"—never
lovers because Poetry was his love and because his emotional involve-
ment was with the bottle—but always "*en rapport*" concerning questions about the world and the self (127).

E. A. believed, according to Mabel, that "some kind of natural
catastrophe was drawing close" (136). Mabel herself was interested in
soothsayers and the occult and went along with Robinson's feeling
that an earthquake or tidal wave would destroy the city of New York.
She is contradictory in calling him "the most inarticulate man I have
ever known" but also recalling how they often "lunched out together,
talking endlessly" (136). "A balancing influence" on her life, E. A.,
Mabel recalls, had keen insights concerning books and people and
events in New York. She took no offense when he criticized Gertrude

Stein's "Portrait of Mabel Dodge," saying he could not take the writer seriously and asking, "How do you know that it is a portrait of you, after all?" (137). Considering all the publicity which both Dodge and Stein had received from her promotion of this little piece, his joking about what had been so serious to her does show Robinson as a balancing influence. No one else had doubted that the portrait was of Mabel, least of all Alice B. Toklas, who would seem to have liked the alternate title, "Mabel little Mabel with her Face against the Pane," presumably a reference to Mabel's inability to enter the sacred precinct occupied by Gertrude and Alice.[7]

Robinson, however, continued to joke about Gertrude, writing Mabel, "I don't know whether G. S. is your aesthetic evil genius, or whether I am a jackass to think that you take her seriously." In company, however, Robinson was usually silent. When Mabel held a poets' evening at her salon, he sat, she remembers, "like a bump on a log and didn't express a thing" (91). Apparently the evening was not so successful as her political or artistic evenings, for Amy Lowell walked out, offended by some verses read by George Sylvester Viereck, and Robinson's silence put the final damper on the occasion. There can be little doubt, however, that Mabel took Robinson to picture galleries, that the two did exchange notes on the books they were reading, and that they held extensive conversations, perhaps because, as Mabel surmises, "I was not academic." All in all Robinson seems to have meant the comment he wrote to Mabel in a letter following their visit to Stieglitz's gallery: "Anyhow I am sure that the world is better and more interesting for your being in it, and that, after all, is the only thing that matters" (138). Although in all his notes to her he signed himself rather formally, "E. A. Robinson," still Mabel seems to have enjoyed a close personal relationship with this great American poet. In any case he seems to have relieved his feelings in letters to her: "The world is a hell of a place, and if life and the universe mean anything, there is no reason to suppose that it will ever be anything else. This, as I understand it, is the true optimism."[8]

Carl Van Vechten

Van Vechten was the music reviewer for the *New York Times* when Mabel met him during her first year in the city. He took his work, she thought, with the same lightheartedness he brought to life itself. His vibrancy and sense of humor animated her otherwise lifeless rooms, creating "an instant response from all those inanimate things" and making the place "alive for us and for all others who ever afterwards entered there" (16). As for Carl, he testified, "I think Mabel had more effect on my life than anybody I ever met."[9] Interestingly enough, writing in 1952, he used almost the same kind of description of Mabel that she had used of him: "By her enthusiasm Mabel makes inanimate things live and gives animate beings a more intense life. Her taste is original and extraordinary. . . . Besides the beauty she has enhanced, it is probable that she has done more to encourage a point of view, if it was only by way of argument, than any one else I have known."[10] One way in which Mabel affected Van Vechten's life was in introducing him to Gertrude Stein, whose work he later edited. Shortly before her death, Stein wrote in a preface to the Modern Library Edition of her *Selected Writings:* "I always wanted to be historical, . . . and Carl was one of the earliest ones that made me certain I was going to be . . . all the time Carl wrote to me and I wrote to him and he always knew, and it was always a comfort."[11]

Mabel also helped Van Vechten by providing the model for a major character for his novel, *Peter Whiffle: His Life and Works* (1922), which presents a young writer, who, having died young, requests in his will that the narrator put him in a novel to compensate for the stories he himself never got written. Some real characters appear in *Peter Whiffle* under their own names—for example, Gertrude Stein, Hutchins Hapgood, Big Bill Haywood—but Mabel appears as Edith Dale, a woman who entertains celebrities in her villa in Florence and at her "evenings" in a Fifth Avenue apartment.

Before the narrator takes Peter Whiffle to one of these affairs, he describes their hostess: "Well, she's a woman, but a new kind of woman, or else the oldest kind; I'm not sure which. . . . She spends her energy in living, in watching other people live, in watching them make their silly mistakes, in helping them make their silly mistakes. She is a dynamo."[12] Edith Dale is further made out to engage in "as many storm centres as possible . . . grasping this faint idea or that frail theory, tossing it back a complete or wrecked formula," and on the other hand to sit silent and withdrawn.[13] In a work of fiction, Van Vechten could be more honest perhaps about the way he looked at Mabel than in journalistic reporting, but he uses so many documented incidents from her actual life and reproduces so accurately some of her letters to him that the novel comes close to biography.

Describing how Edith often sat "like a Madonna," listening without comment, or disappeared from the drawing room, perhaps even to retire to bed, or more often remained in the room "without being present" while the arguments swirled around her, the narrator finds Andrew Dasberg's painting, *The Absence of Edith Dale,* expressive of her ability to perform as catalyst for a group without being involved. Mabel herself considered the abstract painting, *The Absence of Mabel Dodge,* which was "all a flare of thin flames with forked lightnings in them and across the bottom of this holocaust, three narrow black, black, black bars," as Dasberg's expression of anguish for her absence in 1913 when she followed Jack Reed to Texas (249).

Whatever the truth about this picture, Mabel Dodge herself must have seemed like a fictional character to Carl Van Vechten. The decoration of her apartment (green glass, lovely fabrics, and old Italian furniture against the ivory-white of the walls and the hangings), the food she served (tables laden with pinchbottles and Curtis cigarettes by the hundreds, trays of Virginia ham and white Gorgonzola sandwiches, salads, cold meats, and kümmel bottles in the form of Russian bears), and the clothes she wore (lovely gowns of clinging turquoise blue, spinel, and jacinth silks, hats with waving plumes and an avalanche of drooping veils) provided him with many a page of description.

The association of Mabel and Van Vechten was happy, it seems, except for an incident in 1914 when she, Carl, and Neith Hapgood were visiting Florence. Suddenly war was declared, and Carl and Neith, with the Hapgood children and Mabel's son, rushed home to America, abandoning Mabel, who was awaiting the arrival of John Reed at Naples. Although it took her some time to forgive Van Vechten, when Mabel died in 1962 they had been close friends for many years. In paying tribute to her, he may have summed up what others sensed: her "worst quality" was the one that made her great. Carl writes, "She adored to change people. I loved what she did for me and accepted her guidance with pleasure."[14] And she accepted his guidance in turn: late in her life he persuaded Mabel to bequeath her manuscripts and correspondence to the Yale Library, thus preserving a valuable record of aspects of early twentieth-century life.[15]

John Reed

If Carl Van Vechten and Hutchins Hapgood were Mabel's platonic friends, the same cannot be said for the handsome young revolutionary, Jack Reed. A fiery if rather short-lived love affair exploded between them, as they both engaged in the great enterprise of

producing in Madison Square Garden a representation of the bloody
ongoing strike of the silk workers of Paterson, New Jersey. Bill Haywood, head of the International Workers of the World and leader of
the strike for an eight-hour day, could get no New York news coverage of the suffering of the workers or of the violent confrontations
with the police in Paterson. He listened when Mabel suggested pre-
senting the strike in New York, but it was Reed who cried, "I'll do
it," as this "young, big, and full-chested" poet and revolutionary
moved to sit beside her at their first meeting (189).

Mabel thus played many roles during her New York period. A
biographer of Edwin Arlington Robinson calls her "the perceptive
and omnivorous Aspasia of Greenwich Village" who "broke through
the barrier Robinson set up against all women."[16] Whether she can
be compared to Pericles' consort, who supposedly wielded great
power in the intellectual and political circles of Athens, she did break
through many barriers and was involved in the political and artistic
ferment of the prewar years in New York. She was surely more
straightforward than one imagines Aspasia to have been: "in the first
place I wanted to know everybody, and in the second place everybody
wanted to know me. I wanted, in particular, to know the Heads of
things. Heads of Movements. Heads of Newspapers. Heads of all
kinds of groups of people. I became a Species of Head Hunter, in
fact" (83–84). Although Mabel seems to have been unaware of the
cannibalistic connotations of head-hunting which some critics saw in
her, she nevertheless succeeded in this pursuit, even going so far as
to create such Heads as Gertrude Stein in the art world and John
Reed in the political.

The production of the pageant on the night of 7 June 1913, de-
layed by Reed's trip to Paterson, where he was arrested among the
strikers and sentenced to twenty days in prison, made headlines
everywhere when it was produced in Madison Square Garden for an
audience of fifteen thousand. For several frantic weeks, Reed trained
the choir of Paterson men, women, and children to sing many of the
strike songs he composed; he directed and rehearsed the cast of two
thousand, arranged with his Harvard classmate, Robert Edmond
Jones, to design the setting and staging, and obtained John Sloan to
paint the scenery. Although many of the meetings were held at the
home of Margaret Sanger, Mabel herself took credit for the inspired
original suggestion, and for her complete support of Reed during all
the days of planning. "I gave up everything to work on it. Reed was

the executive. I kept having ideas about what to do and he carried them out . . . we were a perfect combination for work—untiring, full of fun, too, and perfectly thrilled by the handful we had taken up" (200).

There was, of course, no time for love between this twenty-five-year-old Harvard poet-writer-revolutionary and the thirty-four-year-old "Man-eating Mabel," as she is called in *The Lost Revolutionary: A Biography of John Reed.*[17] Their relationship consisted of Mabel's "pouring all the power in the universe through myself to him." If he faltered, she explains, "I consciously drew all the force in me into a solid mass like a catapult, and directed it at him" (205). Thus the pageant was created. Without the knowledge of city authorities, Mabel, Reed, and friends managed to construct the letters IWW in bright red electric lights ten feet high on each of the four sides of the Madison Square Garden tower. Under the influence of Gordon Craig, Jones arranged a long street scene right through the audience, so that all were involved in the funeral procession of the martyred striker as it marched to the stage through the crowd. The "pulsing vibration" of the production was recorded next day in the headlines: "Paterson Pageant Packs the Garden," "Hall Blazes with Red and Seethes with Enthusiasm for the 'Cause,' " "I. W. W. Strike Draws 15,000 Audience," "Biggest Cast Ever Seen in a New York Production Stages Its Own Show."

Before the glory could fade, Mabel, Bobby Jones, and Reed sailed for Europe the next day to spend the summer at the Villa Curonia. In Paris, with adjoining rooms, Mabel admitted Reed to her bed in an ecstasy of "all for love and everything else well lost!" "So I came to Reed, then," she writes, "like a Leyden jar, brimful to the edge, charged with a high, electrical force. And this seemed a marvel to him. . . . He whispered to me, that first night: 'I thought your fire was crimson, but you burn blue in the dark' " (216). The days in Paris became "mere interruptions in the labor of passion." Motoring south with Bobby, Reed, and Carl Van Vechten, who had joined them, Mabel wished for the nights when her lover belonged only to her. As Reed roamed about Venice unaware of Mabel, exclaiming, "The things *Men* have done!" she lost her temper, returned to the villa without him, and later quarreled about the value of "what *Men* had done." She, as woman, was a greater creation than anything man had made, and she wanted Reed's recognition of her worth both day and night. Later, when Reed was ill with diphtheria at the villa,

Mabel took pleasure in "complete possession" of his weak body. "A lover sick in bed, one is safe for the moment." A woman is then not defeated by ideas, work, friends, or politics. Depending upon a man "for our sense of identity," she writes, we feel that we are real when he is impotent to do more than gratefully submit to our ministrations. Not surprisingly, the paradoxical feeling that "a man completely at a disadvantage, disempowered, and delivered up to us, we find to be no man at all" gives rise to the question: "Is it possible, then, that one is more satisfied with the struggle than with the surrender?" (229).

During the fall of 1913, Reed and Mabel returned to New York to live openly together. Although Mabel would have liked to discontinue her evenings, Neith and Hutch, Carl, Lincoln Steffens, and others "insisted upon owning me, my house, my life itself, and they all just came along as usual." Another source of frustration was that when Reed perused the morning papers, his imagination pictured events in Mexico or Russia or Poland, in which he might take part, whereas to Mabel "newspapers have never meant anything." Furthermore she contends, "I have never read the news in all my life except when it was about myself or some friend or enemy of mine." (The many scrapbooks of clippings in the Luhan collection at Yale indicate that Mabel not only read the news about herself but saved it.)

Souls as turbulent as Mabel's and Reed's were bound to toss on the seas of emotion. In September 1913, Reed wrote, "You smother me. . . . I am going away to save myself . . . I love you." Mabel fled to the Hapgoods, where she spent a day in tears, then after dinner back to her flat with Walter Lippmann to get her "rusty" mind functioning. She had resolved by morning to live with her loneliness, a fate postponed for the time by Reed's bursting into the room, "pale, with black shadows under his eyes," crying "I missed your love, your selfish, selfish love." Just as she readjusted to having him back, however, Reed accepted an assignment from Carl Hovey to report on Pancho Villa in Mexico for *Metropolitan Magazine,* Mabel following him as far as El Paso before turning back. When Reed returned "The Hero" of the Villa affair, Mabel made much of him and promoted a "Reed in Mexico" evening as well as a talk at the Morristown School, Reed's school, which her son John now attended. In one of her few mentions of her son, Mabel says he took pride in Reed's story of Villa's campaigns and in his gift of the camera used to take the photographs in Reed's book, *Insurgent Mexico* (1914).

Next Reed was off to report on the massacre of striking coal miners by state militia at Ludlow in southern Colorado. His absence led Mabel to speculate that when he was away, she enjoyed her "Evenings," whereas "with Reed at home my power seemed to leave me." Paradoxically torn, as she was so many times throughout her life, she remembers, "I always preferred to have him there and to feel uncertain and unsure of him and of myself rather than to triumph, with him away" (264). The eyes of New Yorkers focused on the chaotic love affair of the most renowned of "The Improper Bohemians," John Reed as the Village Golden Boy and the country's top war correspondent, Mabel Dodge as hostess nonpareil to artistic, social, and political writers and activists of the time.

Reporting on the war in Europe, Reed decried the sordid killing of man by man to no purpose except the support of similar greedy capitalistic states.[18] From this point on, his admiration for socialism increased, only to end with his death in Russia and his burial as a hero close to the Kremlin Wall. Mabel Dodge, apolitical as she was, parted with this heroic revolutionary as his devotion to the unpopular antiwar movement increased.

Mabel concludes the story of Reed with a note of asperity, but with her usual astute vision concerning people, she conveys an impression of him and his wife, Louise Bryant, which rings true:

Finally they went to Russia, like so many others looking for an escape. For Louise it was an opportunity to be on her way, as she wrote quite a good book; for Reed it was adventure again and perhaps a chance to lose himself in a great upheaval. He threw himself into action close to Trotsky and Lenin and when he died of typhus the Russians gave him a splendid public funeral and set a tablet to his memory over his grave, and Louise, draped in crèpe, the wife of a hero, threw herself on his bier long enough to be photographed for the New York papers. (422–23)

Although Reed's fame rested on his story of the Russian Revolution, entitled *Ten Days That Shook the World* (1919), his reporting of the Mexican Revolution, and his death as a Byronic hero in Russia, Mabel knew him first as a poet, the author of a little book of verse, *The Day in Bohemia* or *Life Among the Artists,* published privately in 1913, and consisting of vignettes of Greenwich Village life, some of which she reprinted in *Movers and Shakers* (171–85). To Mabel he wrote poems, one ending, "But the speech of your body to my body will not be denied!" (213), another in the deathlike city of Florence, asking, "Mabel! What are we living things doing here?" and still another called "Pygmalion," in which he depicts himself as Mabel's creator, exclaiming "So Galatea under his kisses stirred."

When Malcolm Cowley reviewed *Movers and Shakers,* he made much of John Reed's place in Mabel's book, titling his piece "Fable for Russian Children" and grossly satirizing Mabel as the wealthy, bourgeois daughter of bankers, whose heart was as "dry and cold as a vault in her father's bank" and who "fell in love with a revolutionary poet and tried to buy him and failed." When she was lonely or idle, he remarked, she "rented a new apartment or bought a house— even if she had many others unoccupied." Still unsatisfied, "she began collecting people in exactly the same spirit as she collected china dogs for her mantlepiece." The revolutionary poet, who "really loved this woman he had brought to life," gets all the best of it. Cowley's only concession to Mabel, on the other hand, is that, "Like any mechanical thing, she was utterly at the mercy of her times."[19]

Max Eastman

During the years Mabel spent in New York, Max Eastmen was editor of the *Masses,* a radical monthly publication that advocated with high good humor rebellion against the status quo and revolution of the working classes. Eastman later recalled, *"The Masses* was such a gay and boisterous magazine, and put so much laughter into revolution, that I seemed to be at the peak of life's enjoyment during it."[20] Although his goals, including that of women's suffrage, were serious, he had the kind of lighthearted spirit that made him see no antagonism between a zeal for improving life and a zest for enjoying it. Although he wrote later, in *Love and Revolution,* that Mabel "always embarrassed me,"[21] still he visited 23 Fifth Avenue, bought a small house near hers when she moved to Finney Farm, north of New York on the Hudson River, and asked her to edit one issue of the *Masses.* He also published several of her pieces in the magazine.

Although he obviously trusted her judgment and ability, he was puzzled by the attraction she had for people. In his book *Enjoyment of Living,* he sums up his life in Bohemia in the early part of the century, trying at one point to explain Mabel's "witchlike fascination" and her notoriety as "a powerful and peculiar collector of intellectuals":

She has neither wit nor beauty, nor is she vivacious or lively minded or entertaining. She is comely and good-natured, and when she says something, it is sincere and sagacious, but for the most part she sits like a lump and says nothing. She seems never to have learned the art of social intercourse—a rather dumb and stumpy little girl, you would say, and move on to someone who at least knew how to make conversation. You would move on just to escape embarrassment, but before long you would be around there trying to talk to this little girl again. For there is something going on, or going round, in Mabel's head or bosom, something that creates a magnetic field in which people become polarized and pulled in and made to behave very queerly. Their passions become exacerbated; they grow argumentative; they have quarrels, difficulties, entanglements, abrupt and violent detachments. And they like it—they come back for more. Many famous salons have been established by women of wit or beauty; Mabel's was the only one ever established by pure will power.[22]

Eastman was much interested in John Reed, who wrote many stories for the *Masses,* and whose love affair with Mabel he closely watched, even fearing that when Reed was off on assignments Mabel seemed to draw closer to Max himself. Perhaps she played something of the mother role to both these young men, so fervent in their idealistic aims. In any case, Eastman portrayed Reed and Mabel in a novel, *Venture* (1927), written six years after the young revolutionary's death, and nearly a decade after the New York hostess had moved to Taos, New Mexico. The story, focusing primarily on Reed (Jo Hancock), also concerns Mabel, fictionalized as Mary Kittridge, playing the role of lover to Hancock and hostess to the literati of New York in a salon much like Mabel's:

Mary Kittridge's house was wide. There were three great windows looking out on a street just East of Fifth Avenue beside the Park. And though these windows were softened and the outdoors gently removed to its place, by a series of warmly-shadowed curtains, nevertheless it was light in Mary's house during the daytime. . . . And the rich and peaceful beauty of the chambers of that house was something that almost seemed to justify the whole labor of civilization.[23]

The drawing room with its perfectly arranged pictures makes it seem possible for one "to rest forever." Expanding Mabel's rooms considerably, he gives his fictional character a library with such comfortable chairs that one could happily spend the whole night, a bedroom that looks out on a delightful back garden fountain, and a sky-lighted studio, where Mary could paint or play the flute. Her dining room at the end of the great drawing room lends "an informal grace" with its beautiful silver and delicious refreshments, similar to that of "a queen's picnic."

Characterized as a romantic poet, Jo "ventures" from the world of business into support of the IWW and the Paterson strike through Mary, whose "zeal for the workers' cause" at first astonishes him. An "evening" at Mary's, the subject of discussion being proletarian art, appropriately led by a character named Bill Haywood is one of the events whereby Mary enlightens the much younger Jo, to whom she is, besides lover, something of a mother and teacher. Eastman's description of the event, with its "joyful assortment of people," indicates that his memories of Mabel are happy ones. "Everybody with special flair for the true or the exotic was there—everybody touched in the head with some wild little sacred excitement or determination about life and how it should be lived."[24] Although it is hardly fair of Eastman to have made Mary old enough to be a friend of Jo's mother, still it reveals how Eastman saw Mabel and perhaps the part she played for him and for Reed.

The part she played in the life of the times, however, he presents with accuracy. "Mary Kittridge was an extravagant person. She was almost as extravagant as the God who made her, and he so loaded her with whims and vigor and talent and money and a thirst after the true meaning of life, that she acquired the renown and popularity of a circus".[25] In exaggerating the number of husbands and lovers and causes she espoused, Eastman nevertheless felicitously describes his semifictional character in terms that fit Mabel: "She waged a perpetual war on habit."[26] Even in making fun of Mary as the instigator of such activities as "the Chinese Theatre Movement, the Revolt against the Art Galleries and the Parlor Car Vaudeville," he accurately portrays her as introducing to the uninitiated the new ideas of the early twentieth century. As in Van Vechten's *Peter Whiffle,* the character closely modeled on Mabel plays the important role in the life of the hero. And if she was "too competitive and aggressive" to be entirely compatible with Eastman, at least "he shared her romantic insistence upon the natural, her obsessive fear of being cut off from 'life!' "[27] Frequenting that popular haunt of intellectuals, the Brevoort Hotel, he would cross the street to Mabel's apartment, where he found continued stimulation of the senses as well as of the mind, which he never forgot.

During Eastman's years as editor of the *Masses* Mabel wrote several vignettes for the publication. "The Secret of War" (November 1914), according to Mabel, is that men like fighting. Writing on her observations in Paris at the time of the declaration of World War I, where she had gone with sober face expecting to experience "the horror of war," she claims, instead, to have found "the whole nation of men, soldiers and officers, happy and excited." The women, however, all stayed in their homes. "The only hope of permanent peace lies in a woman's war against war," which alone can change the light in the eyes of the man she saw transformed by a uniform, "quickened in a way that nothing else has ever quickened him." The essay, whose idea might seem platitudinous, is enlivened by Mabel's keen observation of men setting out to the front. In a nonpolitical account, "The Eye of the Beholder" (October 1917), using fictitious names, Mabel tells the story of how D'Annunizio had made Eleanora Duse an actress, only to unmake her in one night by bringing a new love with him to the theater where she was playing. When she no longer felt herself to be a great actress in the eye of the beholder, she ceased to be one.

Besides including several other short essays, Eastman asked Mabel, "Will you take over April or May (1914) number of *The Masses?*" adding the inducement, "Will advertise you as editor of the issue" (154). Mabel's name was well enough known to improve the circulation of a magazine under her editorship, and Eastman's confidence was great enough to allow her "unconditional freedom of expression." Since he was sometimes annoyed by her affectation and critical of her domineering ways, his offer is more telling evidence of her ability and popularity than the testimony of her close friends, Hapgood and Van Vechten.[28]

Alfred Stieglitz and the International Exhibition of Modern Art

Besides her many relationships with writers and political journalists, Mabel was a mover in the realms of painting, sculpture, music, drama, and dance. In close touch with modern movements in Florence, she brought with her to New York a sophisticated understanding of continental art. It is no wonder, then, that although she was not responsible for originating the idea of the famous art exhibit which opened on 17 February 1913 at the Sixty-ninth Regiment Armory in New York, her enthusiasm and support added to the success of undoubtedly the most sensational exhibit of the early century and perhaps of all time in America. The show consisted of 1,600 paintings, drawings, and sculptures, some of them by the most daring innovators of the time, arranged in the eighteen rooms into which the great hall of the armory had been divided. The show was instigated by a group of progressive artists of the time, urged on by photographer Alfred Steiglitz, whose gallery at 291 Fifth Avenue was an exhibition and gathering place for new American artists. Mabel often visited "291" and thoroughly approved of Stieglitz's encouragement of young artists and of his claim for photography as an art in his publication, *Camera Work* (1915) (which also contained poems, including Mabel's "The Mirror").

"Explosive" was the word used, even fifty years later, for the famous Armory Show, which had an unprecedented attendance of 4,000 on opening night and 100,000 paid admissions during its month at the armory, and many more at its subsequent showing in Chicago and Boston.[29] For the first time Cezanne, Gauguin, Van Gogh, Picasso, Matisse, and Duchamp with his *Nude Descending a Staircase* received wide exposure in America. Everyone from taxi drivers to important industrialists had opinions about the exhibit, many of them hostile to the new kind of nonrepresentational art. It was as if the sponsors, having set out to demonstrate a new invention called the wheel, were run over by something called an automobile; in Chicago some of them were burned in effigy, and in Boston the reaction was hardly less violent.

Mabel, though not one of the instigators, was propelled to fame: "With the close of the Armory Show, Mabel Dodge found herself a minor celebrity. People began to call at 23 Fifth Avenue unexpectedly."[30] Her principal contributions to the Armory Show had been five hundred dollars, the use of her chauffeur and limousine for errands, personal persuasion of various wealthy New Yorkers to lend pictures, and an important article on Gertrude Stein in the special issue of *Arts and Decoration* (March 1913), published in connection with the show, publicizing Stein and identifying herself as a sympathetic interpreter of experimental art forms. So widely was she recognized that when Stieglitz the next year published *Camera Work 47*

(July 1914), a compilation of what his gallery had meant to sixty-eight different writers, Mabel Dodge's answer to "What is 291?" was the opening piece in the issue.[31]

Mabel is correct, as W. G. Rogers points out, in claiming that "the show certainly did gain by my propulsion." An effusive letter of thanks from Arthur Davies, head of the exhibition committee, and her election as vice-president of the affair "testify to her important services."[32] Carl Van Vechten exaggerated Mabel's role in his novel, *Peter Whiffle,* making Edith Dale "set about, quite spontaneously, arranging for the first great exhibition of the post-impressionistic and cubist painters in New York." Still, her intangible influence on the Armory Show and on "291" was greater than could be documented in fact, and powerful enough to inspire fiction.

Isadora Duncan and the Duncan School of Dance

More revolutionary even than the graphic art of the time was the dancing of Isadora Duncan and the school for girls founded by Elizabeth and Isadora Duncan, which taught the free-flowing self-expression of the body. Van Vechten described Isadora's dancing of the "Marseillaise": "Part of the effect is gained by gesture, part by the massing of her body, but the greater part by facial expression. . . . She does not make a sound . . . but the hideous din of a hundred raucous voices seems to ring in our ears."[33] Mabel, entranced by Isadora's performances in New York, described her as "the most truly living being I had ever seen." She made one know "the splendid and terrible potentialities one bore within oneself." Further testifying to Isadora's power, Mabel writes, "I have seen her do a maenad's dance in *Eurydice* when her hair seemed to turn into coiling serpents, . . . and the cataclysmic violence of the demon struck up through her, appearing to rend her cell from cell" (333).

With no funds, but with an unquenchable belief in their method of training children's bodies to move with pure beauty, Elizabeth and Isadora Duncan persuaded Mabel to buy them a studio building and house on beautiful Mt. Airy near Croton-on-Hudson north of New York City, below which Mabel herself purchased a smaller house. She withdrew her son John "from the atmosphere of the stuffy boarding school" and "gave him to Elizabeth Duncan." As a little Greek archer, he took part in the transport of Mt. Olympus to Mt. Airy, just as the sisters had brought Greek dance to America.

Mabel later leased nearby Finney Farm for herself and, disenchanted with causes and petitioners, gave up 23 Fifth Avenue, thus partaking of the simpler life that the sisters espoused. Her establishment of the school at Croton in 1914 had made a great contribution to the support of the Duncans in their effort to bring expressionistic dance to America, and Mabel's recording of the surrounding events, such as the one in which Isadora insulted New York Mayor Pumoy Mitchell, adds an important footnote to its history (324–29).

Maurice Sterne: Painter or Sculptor?

When in 1917 Mabel Dodge married Maurice Sterne, the reactions among her friends ranged from disbelief to sorrow. Leo Stein had written in regard to a possible marital arrangement between Mabel and Maurice: "Now, my dear Mabel, I really like you far too much to have any patience with your making an ass of yourself." He concluded the letter, "Once more, don't be an idjut" (413). Hazel Albertson, a close woman friend, had written in like vein: "It would be a mad thing to do. Perfectly mad. . . . Your rhythms are totally different" (395). When Mabel and Maurice took the step that "had been alluring and repelling us for so long," only a nun, Sister Beatrix, who had a school in Nyack across the river from Finney Farm, seemed to rejoice, for the knowledge of them as unwed lovers had distressed her. Hutchins Hapgood, in trying to be kind, revealed his doubts: "I hope it will solve all your problems—and not make Maurice's more difficult." Dr. A. A. Brill, Mabel's psychiatrist, likewise tried to be ameliorative after the fact: "My objections were purely academic. I never said I disapproved but I counseled waiting a bit longer." Arthur Brisbane wrote, "I do not think it was a very good idea for you to get married. . . . If you continue writing, you will of course not change the signature to your articles" (530).

Elizabeth Duncan added to the chorus with, "Whatever did you do *that* for? . . . I never thought much of marriage myself. Isadora always called it 'that dirty trick.' " Suffragist Marie Howe, who lived in a house below Finney Farm, lectured Mabel: "You have shown women they had the *right* to live as they chose to live and that they do not lose respect by assuming that right. But *now!* When I think of the *disappointment* in the whole women's world today!" When Robert Edmond Jones silently arrived at the farm, "He brought a bunch of hot-house flowers with him and he looked as though he had come to a funeral." Worst of all, Mabel's young son, John, "felt Maurice was detrimental to him, lowering his self-respect." As Mabel remembers it, "There wasn't a single happy word given to me over the affair. . . . My conventional friends hated it and my unconventional ones did too!" (528).

The obvious question is, why did Mabel and Maurice Sterne get married? The answer is not easy to identify, for Mabel hated Sterne's cigars, resented his making her burn Reed's letters, saw him as "full of nervous fears," a self-made man who lacked the background that several generations of cultured family give and as "an apple that is rotted before it is ripe." Yet it was she who, after rejecting his proposals many times, suggested suddenly that they marry, whereafter, without even a honeymoon night, she sent him on the vacation trip he was planning to the West. Mabel's attempt at self-analysis in autobiographical volumes is perhaps accurate—in concluding that she "seized upon this man, determined to change his whole scheme of work": that is, to make him a sculptor instead of a painter.

When she first saw an exhibit of Sterne's paintings of the natives of Bali, where he had lived for a year, she announced to the director of the gallery that the artist "was a sculptor, not a painter." She seems to have felt that Maurice, who spent much time lounging in the apartment lent him by Nazimova (the famous actress and his former lover), would be less sedentary as a sculptor and also that his painting was "sculpturesque, plastic, three-dimensional," like sculpture, but "ugly in color," an unfortunate attribute in paintings. Perhaps with a plan of action already in mind, Mabel bought a small painting, after which Sterne, predictably, showed up at Croton. "Nothing," writes Mabel, "stimulates an artist's interest in one quite so much as having one buy something of his."

In the course of their rocky love affair, she pleads, "Maurice, let me order some clay for you. Try modeling. It seems to me your hands just long to handle some solid substance." He replies, "I know I can make form as plastic with paint as a sculptor does with clay" (433). At another time she summarizes her intent: "I would light a real fire in him before I was through: when I had him malleable I would make him throw away his yellow green paint and take to clay" (369).

As a matter of fact, Maurice Sterne had studied sculpture with Rodin in Paris and had on display in the Brooklyn Museum a modeled

head, but now preferred painting and hence rejected Mabel in the
role which she described as that of "a superior and spiritual mother
who was trying to shape unwieldy material into an image that would
be more pleasing." Even in his lovemaking, Mabel relates, "His
strong, rather bland hands traveled over me, sizing up shapes, as
sculptors' hands are made to do." But still her scheme to change the
course of his career failed, and her drowsy murmur of " 'I think you
were meant to be a sculptor,' " was drowned out by his egotistical pan-
egyric upon his visual capacities. Talk of marriage between them usually ended up with his pleading for Mabel's help in stabilizing his
life, she replying, " 'Well, Maurice, you are a natural *sculptor*. You
shouldn't be trying to paint.' " As Mabel describes the situation:
"Maurice and I continued to play with the idea of marriage in much
the same way that one pokes at a snake with a stick" (394). Apparently it tantalized them both with its danger, which they still found
irresistible.

No matter what Mabel thought of Sterne as a painter, she insisted
one summer on Cape Cod that he paint the portrait of her that he
had long ago suggested. He sulkily began to draw, "took the plunge
he had been nervously postponing" and, through the days she posed,
completed the series called "Portraits of Mabel Dodge"; these according to Mabel, were "exhibited that winter in New York with so
much success and with so much talk of masterly draughtmanship"
(389). Pleased with his use of single tubes of blue or sanguine, Mabel
liked the series, which were indeed praised by the critics and purchased by a number of buyers. But still she wanted him to try
sculpture.

Twenty years after the events, Mabel tries to analyze the love-hate
relationship that tied them in bonds they would like to break: "How
I irked him! . . . Whenever his life moved in him, I checked it because I could not let him be himself. . . . I must raise him and make
him different." She also writes accusingly, "Well, if I hampered him,
how he limited me, too! . . . when one has been caught up by one
like Maurice, it is as if so little of one's energy can be poured out
that most of one's energy is dammed up and sent coursing backwards,
poisoning one throughout and driving one mad" (429).

Sterne, writing many years later, likewise expressed paradoxical
feelings about Mabel. "She might have been a fortuneteller. She
looked like one, dressed like one, and created that kind of atmos-

phere." Although she "courageously followed her impulses" as when she promoted Gertrude Stein, still she had "no vitality or creative power of her own." To Sterne "she was a dead battery who needed constantly to recharge with the juice of some man." Her memoirs, in which he was characterized as a lazy, mediocre artist, relieved Mabel's "ache to be doing something 'significant,' " he concluded, and also promoted what she cared about most, her own glory.[34]

When Mabel and Sterne were together, they quarreled. When they were apart, he wrote her daily loving letters, a number of which she includes in *Movers and Shakers*. Mabel tries to put in words her complicated feelings about her lover: "To ponder upon Maurice's nature was like gazing at night onto the oily black surface of a restless ocean where phosphorescence, bunched here and there within it, breaks up the glassy opaqueness. . . . One never knew where one was with him. Yet the strange part of it was that the man fascinated me by his form. His expression in gestures and looks had a certain round completeness, his body had mass." (414).

Compared to John Reed, Maurice had "a dignity in his European decay that impressed me more than Reed's, or any other American's, budding culture. If Maurice was over-ripe, Reed was too green—or so it seemed to me when I compared them." Sterne was at home only in the crowded flat of his old mother who, in "the hot black wig of Yiddish widowhood," cooked "the food of his childhood," whereas Reed was at home in the world.

It was Maurice Sterne, however, whom Mabel impulsively married on 18 August 1917, in a notary public's office. In the evening, Mabel writes, "I felt terribly alone . . . out on the porch, I in the hammock and Maurice in the big rocking-chair." In spite of this unpromising beginning, however, Maurice's letters from Wyoming, and later from New Mexico, in which he described the Indian people of Santa Fe, inflamed her imagination and radically affected the course of Mabel's life. Although she had forced him to take the trip without her, she responded to the picture his letters evoked by one night having a vision of an Indian face "with wide-apart eyes that stared at me with a strong look, intense and calm." Thus in her dream the frightening face of Sterne was replaced by the medicinal one of the Pueblo Indian Tony Luhan, long before she met Luhan in person, forecasting, as the mystical Mabel saw it, a new life in the West, and the end of her close association with the Movers and Shakers of the East.

The Search For Self

In part 2 of *Movers and Shakers,* entitled "For Maurice Sterne the Sculptor," Mabel reveals her further struggle for selfhood. Two chapters in this section bear the names of Mabel's psychiatrists, "Dr. Jelliffe" and "Dr. Brill." In some sense all her writing originated in the doubtless not unusual motivation of her need for therapy. Although her work was first recognized as a memoir, a genre which focuses "not on the narrating self, but rather on the outer world of people and events," it is of even greater interest as autobiography, a genre which "narrates the story of a person's unfolding sense of identity," usually involving "considerable self-analysis on the part of the author."³⁵ Useful as Mabel's memories of important people have been to historians and biographers, her remarkable struggle for selfhood as a woman particularly interests us today.

As an enthusiast for the new science of psychoanalysis, she reveals its weaknesses as well as its benefits to her. Although Maurice Sterne joined her in some of the sessions, his enthusiasm was not great, and once when she had sent him to Pottsville, Pennsylvania, to paint in the mountains, he wrote in his daily letter to her: "How long do you think your psychoanalysis will take: It just occurred to me that since most of the trouble between us began when you started the course, it would perhaps be advisable that I stay here until you are through with it" (450). He resented Mabel's "laying bare on the psychoanalytical operating table" the secret life between them and feared that she would lose what makes her unique, a "fundamental *honesty* and *truthfulness.*" He feared that digging too deeply in the past would nullify the present. Mabel, however, who had always had some belief in mystics, soothsayers, manifestations from the dead, and her own psychic powers, sought help from psychoanalysts as a more scientific means of getting at her intuitive nature.

She had tried other things: discussions at her evenings, country life at Finney Farm, a more private life at an apartment on Washington Square decorated all in white like the one on Fifth Avenue, and finally even the acquisition of a child. Deciding that perhaps she was tired of "trying to be emancipated," and that she had "been too occupied with another kind of emotion" to have had any feeling for John as a infant, she sought a baby to adopt. The youngest child she could get, a pretty little orphan, nine-year-old Elizabeth, whom she dressed in all sorts of frilly drawers and petticoats with colored ribbons, satisfied Mabel for a while, but she soon turned the child over to the Duncans. "The solidarity between a woman and a baby" which Mabel longed to feel, "this nourishing and reassuring congress," was never to be hers.

Mabel sometimes wondered if what she most needed was not a strong man who would take the responsibility for all decisions. "I wanted to lie back and float," she writes, "on the dominating decisive current of an all-knowing, all-understanding man." The only man she knew who might qualify was Walter Lippmann, a friend she turned to often and held in her imagination as an ideal male. Lacking a close relationship with a "man who would act like a man," Mabel, to fill the vacuum in her life, created by the absence of child, lover, or causes, read mystical books, such as the writings of the Saints, Plotinus, the Rosicrucians, and Gurdieff. Then she was in touch with a Christian Science healer, a smiling, blue-eyed woman with gray hair who came to give her treatments which lightened Mabel's spirits temporarily, after which "the heaviness and the darkness" always returned. Friends were often not available when she needed them. "I had lost the world," she declares. "The world never gives one up. It is something in oneself that gives it up. The instant one relaxes one's fingers, everything slips away. . . . There is no cohesion apart from one's own coherence" (311–12).

An early exponent of Freudian analysis in the prewar years in New York was Dr. A. A. Brill, who, when he came to lead the discussion at one of Mabel's evenings, had caused several guests to walk out, "incensed at his assertions about unconscious behavior and its giveaways." Her more old-fashioned psychiatrist, Dr. Bernard Sachs, had refused to attend, advising Mabel of the danger of Freudian ideas, just as he had advised that modern art at the Armory Exhibit made clear that many of the artists should be restrained in a psychopathic ward. Feeling very abandoned and lonely at Finney Farm a few years later, she turned to Dr. Brill, who became convinced that the activity of 23 Fifth Avenue, with its movements and leagues and exhibits and discussions was what Mabel needed, contrary to her opinion that the sweet williams and pheasants on the land brought her comfort. "To appease Brill, and get him off the idea of my return to town," Mabel confides, between August 1917 and February 1918 she wrote each week for Arthur Brisbane's *New York Journal* two or three light, short fictional pieces she calls *feuilletons,* which were also syndicated through the other Hearst newspapers.

The *feuilletons* showed evidence of the Freudian psychology that she was learning from Brill, popularized for the taste of her readers. In 1936 she had written: "Looking back upon it now, it seems as though everywhere, in that year of 1913, barriers went down and people reached each other who had never been in touch before; there were all sorts of new ways to communicate, as well as new communications" (39). Mabel's importance today is evidenced by the number of historians who have found her commentary apt.[36] Her importance at the time of writing for the *Journal* was that, although she never mentioned Freud, she gave wider circulation to some of his ideas than did professional journalists in less widely read publications.

Her commentary in "Mothers of Men" (13 September 1917) warned that although mothers are the bearers of sons, they may be the destroyers as well, pulling the grown male back to the childhood comforts of the maternal bosom. Without mentioning the Oedipus complex she conveys a quite anti-Victorian view of the dominating mother whose son can never mature into manhood. Did Mabel herself, perhaps, recognize this role as one she played with Reed and Sterne? At the same time she was writing the columns, she was planning and decorating Sterne's studio in New York because he "was incapable of doing it himself," and building another in her orchard which she kept supplied with fresh flowers for his canvases. Earlier she had taken just such a protective role toward Reed, from which he had had difficulty in escaping. In "Men and Girls, Spend All Energy Well" (2 December 1917), she again warned women against smothering their children and husbands with misplaced love and urged that energy be expended in avocations like writing and painting.

On the other hand, in "Women Who Seek Masters" (28 August 1917) she defined the truly mature woman as one who is "free and alone, in the brotherhood of man, bearing her own soul." Perhaps again writing from some recognition of her own feeling of need for a dominant male, she describes the more hopeful state in which a woman depends upon herself alone. Thus, as she concludes in "The Crime of Stealing Energy" (31 October 1917), men and women should not take life from one another but rather should release their energy and their love to one another. In "Sickness Is a Failure of Your Mind" (10 January 1918), she perhaps shows more influence of Christian Science than of Freud, but in "Love Is A Big Energy Dynamo" (9 December 1917) she seems to refer to Freud's libido, the basic life energy, as she saw it, of which everything in civilization is a symbol.

"On the Unconscious" also describes in Freudian terms the land where lie "the obscure laws of our being which if we could but read them would save us from madness and death."

Mabel also expressed her opinions on sociological subjects, which had been discussed at her evenings. Socialism would not improve man's lot, she judged, unless rulers learned through self-control not to repeat the crimes of the past. In "Growth of Love" (14 August 1917), she wrote idealistically of the development of love through the steps of self-love and love of objects, to finally the love of humanity, the object of mature growth.[37] She proposed that even men like Lincoln Steffens, long agreeing with Marx that the class system was the root of social injustice, came to see in that other great influential mind, Sigmund Freud's, another kind of effort to "tear away the suffocating layers of bourgeois culture that strangled physical and creative human expression." And if "Steffens was more interested in the social and political implications of psychoanalysis than in the unleashing of his own passions," still he may have learned through some of Mabel's evenings or her writing that his earlier muckraking did not take account of man's psychological drives.[38] Although Mabel's little expositions may not be worth reprinting in themselves, this "godmother of the Intelligentsia," as Oscar Cargill sees her, had great influence on her times.[39]

If Mabel went to psychoanalysis "when she felt bored or in need of a confirmation of her own prejudices," still she helped to make Americans conscious of new ways of looking at human nature. Like Stieglitz, who saw art "not as a *divertissement,* a refuge from the world, but as a bridge to new consciousness of self, to life," so she saw, not only art, but the science of interpretation of the mind through psychiatry. Stieglitz's purpose had been "to procure America what she most needs—self-consciousness."[40] Mabel's purpose likewise was to bring to a lay public a knowledge of ways in which to examine the self. She agreed that analysis was a kind of tattletaling: "I was able," she writes, "to tell not only everything about myself but all about Maurice." Her aim nevertheless was to improve their relationship through understanding, an aim in which she encouraged his participation.

Besides the Freudian, Dr. Brill, Mabel went for a considerable period three times a week to the Jungian psychiatrist, Dr. Smith Ely Jelliffe, who convinced her that the psyche rebels when forced into a path antipathetic to its nature. He also taught her that a set of symbols define the human body, the respiratory organs standing for human aspiration, the very breath of God. Dr. Jelliffe, who had written a book on the somatic, the psychic, and the symbolic levels of human functioning, had, according to Mabel, "a speculative mind with an amusing intuition." He turned her "starved perceptions," which had been concentrated on Sterne, in the new direction of self-examination, "more and more upon the inner workings of my own nature."

"Often what we think we find in others is nothing but our own hidden life," he advised. Mabel as she recounts it was astonished. Must she track down the Maurice in herself? "Was I attached to *myself* instead of to him as I supposed?" she asks. Reasoning further, she concludes that if unadmirable characteristics which she sees in another are really in her, perhaps the reverse is also true, that the admirable characteristics which she sees in a friend like Walter Lippman are also within her. A reviewer for the Catholic magazine *Commonweal,* after condemning "the paganism of her circle," disparaged Mabel's psychological speculations: "There is something at once repellant and pathetic about this egocentric heiress who lolls back in her white bed, hung with purest Chinese silk, reading about mysticism and interspersing the chronicle of her lusts with the patter of Freud.[41]

In some matters Mabel Dodge seems to have had great assurance that her own way was the one to follow; in others she felt insecure and ill-defined. She had not hesitated to take John Reed as lover, to be among the first to bob her hair and put off the restricting corsets of her debutante days; yet she felt the need of psychiatric help to resolve her inner turmoil. In some respects she sounds very modern: "New York was largely run by women; there was a woman behind every man in every publisher's office, in all the editorial circles, and in the Wall Street offices," but these women seemed to be content to function anonymously (143). The Heterodoxy Club, however, was composed of women whose names were known and whom Mabel found to be "joyous and independent" human beings, but unlike them she could not dedicate herself to the cause of improved industrial relations or women's suffrage or any of the other rights espoused by women like Charlotte Perkins Gilman, Mary Fels, Edna Kenton, Mary Heaton Vorse, or Fola La Follette.

In spite of being honored wherever she lived for her domestic arts, and for playing hostess to innumerable guests who enjoyed the company as well as the sumptuous refreshments, she felt incomplete in this woman's role. At Finney Farm, she says, "I felt terribly lonely and empty in that large, quiet house where all the life was going on in the kitchen, a place I seldom entered." As at the Villa Curonia, she disavowed all knowledge of and interest in the preparation of food, which lent a life to the kitchen that was lacking in her own chambers. There seems to have been nowhere that Mabel felt complete and at ease. One reviewer called *Movers and Shakers* "the portrait of a stranger in the world." As she put it, "The puzzle of my life lacked parts." Never could she find the missing pieces in Buffalo, in Florence, or in New York. Now nearly forty years old, however, events led her strangely to the West, to New Mexico, where, if she never found them all, at least she located on the edge of Taos Desert some of those pieces which her life had lacked.

Chapter Four

Westering—The Broken Life Line: *Edge of Taos Desert* and *Winter in Taos*

Taos and the Pueblo Indians

The source of the title of Mabel Dodge's last book of memories of her life and the epigraph for it came, surprisingly enough, from an *East* Indian proverb, although the volume *Edge of Taos Desert* (1937) is largely concerned with the Pueblo Indians of New Mexico and Mabel's reaction to the new land. The proverb, "He who loves with passion lives on the edge of the desert," Mabel found fitting, metaphorically no doubt because of her deep love for the country and for the person of Anthony Lujan (Tony Luhan), and literally because of the high desert stretching out beyond Taos, which itself rests at the foot of the Indians' Sacred Taos Mountain of the Sangre de Cristo Range. Wheeler Peak, at over 13,000 feet, is the highest point in the range and in New Mexico, and hence rises protectively behind Taos Pueblo, which is three miles closer than Taos to "the half-circle of mountains which surrounds the somnolent desert and embraces the oasis that is named Taos."[1]

At the urging of Maurice Sterne, who had joined other artists in Santa Fe, Mabel in December of 1917 took the train to this small New Mexico town without great enthusiasm. Although Sterne expected her to feel at home in his small adobe house, she impulsively departed for Taos, taking Maurice and her son John, who had joined them for Christmas vacation. The owner of a small hotel and a Ford car, a Mr. Craft, agreed to take the three up the seventy-five miles of frozen, winding, deeply rutted road to Taos, a town of a few settlers of which Mabel had only vaguely heard and which the driver had only visited once. Even before the end of the journey, the magic of the land bewitched this sojourner from Eastern cities. At Embudo, a narrow-gauge train stop with a solitary station and lunch building, Mabel breathed the thin, cold air and cried out:

"Holy! Holy! Holy!" I exclaimed to myself. "Lord God Almighty!" I felt a sudden recognition of the reality of natural life that was so strong and so unfamiliar that it made me feel unreal. I caught a fleeting glimpse of my own spoiled and distorted nature, seen against the purity and freshness of these undomesticated surroundings. (32–33)[2]

In spite of the cold, the difficult journey, the lack of good food, and the foreign nature of the few people they met, she was ecstatic:

It was intensely silent out there without a stirring of anything; and yet I seemed to hear, inside the silence, a high, continuous humming, like a song; and it made my happy. For the first time in my life I heard the world singing in the same key in which my own life inside me had sometimes lifted and poured itself out. But that had been a solitary thrill before this. Now the world and I were met together in the happiest conjunction. Never had I felt so befriended. (32)

Waxing ecstatic at another time, Mabel listened to the "high, humming silence of a lonely winter countryside in one of the altitudes of the earth":

The air is very thin and seems to be more penetrable than the denser ones of the lowlands, and it is as though all kinds of ethereal essences and elementary perceptions creep through from beyond our usual plane and we become aware of the life in things—in trees, and rivers—and there are curious messages, only half received, borne to us on the movement of the winds. (99)

Not only nature, but the Indians as well, furnished a new experience. As she listened to the communal chanting from nearby Taos Pueblo, with its many adobe houses built like children's blocks upon one another, she was enthralled:

For the first time in my life, then, I heard the voice of the One coming from the Many—I who until then had been taught to look for the wonders of infinite divisibility and variety, for the many in the one, the elaboration and detail of a broken infinity. My world, all through my life, had been made of parts ever increasingly divided into more intricate and complex fractions. By our contemplation of pieces of things we had grown to believe that the part is greater than the whole; and so division had motivated all the activities of people I had known, of books I had read, of music I had heard, and of pictures I had seen. (62–63)

The Pueblo Indians, according to anthropologist Ruth Benedict, have "a civilization whose forms are dictated by the typical choices of the Apollonian, all of whose delight is in formality and whose way of life is the way of measure and sobriety." Their sense of "man's oneness with the universe" means that they do not picture the universe in dualistic terms of good and evil. . . . "Life is always present, death is always present. Death is no denial of life. The seasons unroll themselves before us, and man's life also."[3] The Pueblos take little stock in heroism and prowess, honoring rather the man of generous heart with no suspicion of arrogance or strong emotion. The tribe as a whole is what matters. Each individual, sharing his breath with the breath of the Gods, is in harmony with the universe.

With remarkable acuity Mabel seems to have thoroughly understood or at least appreciated the virtues of the Pueblos and to feel more and more removed from the urban culture of her past. In spite of the primitive housing, unlettered white inhabitants, Mexican Penitentes of a Dionysian bent, the dubious ability of the one doctor, the questionable business ethics of their landlord, and the general lack of cultural atmosphere and comfortable living conditions, Mabel decided to remain in Taos.

Maurice and John in Taos

Since Maurice Sterne was part of the old life, Mabel's attachment to him, hardly strong to begin with, was bound to weaken. As the high, dry air of the mountains and admiration of the Pueblo way of life enveloped her, she resented the restrictions of marriage and encouraged him to return to New York alone. Feeling as she did about her own renewal, however, she was sad that he must go back to experience only the time-worn old. "I knew to what world he was returning," she writes. "I felt I had been delivered from it and that he was still condemned" (320). Hardly even crediting him with being the cause of her deliverance from the settled world and its psychiatrists, she nevertheless felt regret that Sterne must face what she had left behind. She writes: "I somehow knew that I would never have to pretend to be a part of that old world again and that the need to conform to that environment, as Brill had tried to teach me to do, was really not a necessary exercise" (320).

Of her four marriages, that to Maurice Sterne, puzzling to her friends and even to herself, had the revolutionary effect of placing her in a completely compatible environment. It seems also to have been the one in which her son John was most involved. It was Sterne on his lonely honeymoon trip who first informed the sixteen year old at the Rumseys' ranch in Wyoming of this union whereby the husband became an unwelcome stepfather to the boy. It was Sterne who had to care for John when he arrived in Santa Fe from Cody at Christmas time with no money, ahead of the arrival of his mother. And it was Sterne who experienced some rivalry there with the boy for the attention of the mother-wife, who practiced a certain coquetry, as if with the intent of creating ill-feeling between them.

The freedom Mabel felt in this isolated place, in the rented rooms of part of a large adobe house owned by a Mr. Manby, a long-time white resident and speculator, caused her suddenly to ask John to cut her hair, which now was long with huge braided coils over the ears. John lovingly clipped and clipped, straight across the eyebrows and down just below the ears. When Mabel had once impulsively cut her hair as a girl in Buffalo, her father had raged and her mother had made her wear a switch, so that any freedom she had hoped to attain at that time had been frustrated. This time, when Mabel wondered what Sterne would say, John replied truculently that it was none of his business and wished that Maurice were permanently absent.

On the one hand Mabel wanted her son and husband to be friends; on the other, when they "seemed to get along better than before," she resented their lack of attention to her. Neither John nor Sterne approved of Mabel's going to Taos Pueblo to teach the Indian girls the household art of knitting, as she did each morning, walking the two to three miles from the back of Manby's dwelling to the Indian village, between breakfast and lunch. John told her he thought the Indians must think her very strange, and Sterne was sure she was wasting her time if she hoped to teach the Indian girls any useful arts.

As for Mabel, "More and more," she writes, "I felt my real home was in the Pueblo. . . . it was like entering into a new dimension" (174), and both John and her husband found other occupations which prevented their noticing how Mabel occupied her time. Sterne, taking an Indian girl as model and cook, and her brother to hunt game, went up in the hills to one of the abandoned miner's cabins, where he happily brushed on thin layers of wax as he modeled the girl and smoked on the porch in the evening while the boy played his drum and the sun set beyond the mountains.

It was the separateness of the people of Taos from each other, perhaps illustrated by her own family, that made Mabel admire the Indians' group life. Among the whites, "everyone was entirely different from everyone else, in taste, activity, and interest," and "everyone was deeply lonely and negative in loneliness." Among the Indians on the other hand was a gentle feeling of cohesion. In their chants the Indians spoke with one voice, in a timbre that vibrated in Mabel's soul. With Sterne in his own studio in Taos and John much occupied "with his own concerns," it was inevitable that she turned to the Indians and particularly to Tony Luhan. Even though Sterne was now interested in sculpture, as she had wanted, Mabel was no longer interested in him, and hence his depature was imminent. Although he too had been able to respond to the group dancing and chanting of the Indians—"How it smoothens one out!" he had exclaimed—and according to Mabel, "was not so dead or so ruined as others I knew," still he could not engage in the mystical communion of the Indians which was "as natural and inevitable as the communion between the cells of the body, and similar to that" (66). Although she had been content through life to obtain more than an average share of *things,* such as draperies, porcelain, and silver, Mabel was now sensing that the white man was "weighted down with all the accretions of our civilization: the buildings and machinery, the multitudinous objects we had invented and collected about us, and ourselves fairly buried under the heavy load, muffled, stifled, going under" (197). When Sterne suggested that it was time to return to New York, Mabel made it clear that he was an "accretion" unnecessary for her happiness and would have to return alone.

Mabel and Tony

Since Mabel had seen, before leaving New York, an apparition of a dark, calm Indian face with green leaves surrounding it, an apparition that brought her surcease from the frightening dream before it, she did not consider it strange that Tony Luhan had also seen her face in a vision before they met. Such magical appearances are granted to those who truly love. When Tony told her just how she wore her hair in coils over the ears, although she wore it cut the first time he saw her, Mabel knew that they had been fated for each other long before they met. Two souls of different races called to each other across the continent, and Mabel responded by leaving the harried life of the East Coast and taking up the gentle, passive life of the centuries-old culture of the Tiwa tribe of Pueblo Indians.

Almost before they were settled in their rooms at Taos, Mabel persuaded John to drive her and Maurice to Taos Pueblo, where a beautiful Indian woman, wearing a black cotton dress sprigged with white and a broad red woven belt wound twice around to support her deep bosom, graciously invited them into her house. With only a tiny high window affording any light, it was some moments before they could see the rolls of blankets against the white-washed walls and a man with a drum who was softly chanting by the fireplace. Astonishingly, when the singer finally raised his head and looked at Mabel "with a quick glance that penetrated to the depths with an instantaneous recognition," she saw the face of her dream, "the same face, the same eyes, involuntarily intense, with the living fire in their depths" (94). It did not strike her as ironic that the Indian woman who had invited them in to hear the song was Tony's wife, Candelaria, nor that it was her husband Maurice, appearing uncomfortable in the adobe Indian home, who had brought her to Taos.

Maurice had come as an artist. As time wore on, however, the more he exclaimed about the Indian art which was real and all their own, the more Mabel began to tell herself that it was the Indian *life* that was real, "and deep as fate, and full of wisdom and experience." Nobody among the Indians asked her questions, as her family did when she got home. There was an ease and naturalness to the Indian way of life that made her feel she was in "a new dimension" whenever she had crossed the fields and entered the Indians' homes. Through Tony Luhan's rapt appreciation of the natural world, her senses were sharpened to new voices of the wind outside and of the crackling fire to which she had been blind and deaf. And in the closely crowded Taos Pueblo, where one room stood upon another and families were crowded into small spaces, Mabel never heard any angry words, "only courteous and dignified exchange between neighbors." There was even "a honey sweetness in their daily bread that I never knew in mine." Their natural acceptance of life transferred itself to the very food they ate. So Mabel writes, "When I trudged back home, down the road . . . and over the two little bridges that crossed the gay, small, sparkling Pueblo creek that came tumbling from the sacred mountain, my heart was not so full of anticipation as on my journey out" (177). At home neither the food nor the life was so sweet.

As the spring wore on into summer, Mabel writes, "The stream of my life was flowing towards Tony." When he offered to take her and Maurice on a day's trip through the neighboring hamlets across the desert to a hot spring, she and her husband sat behind while Tony talked about the sights along the way with the young Indian Pete, who had modeled for Maurice. Mabel wore her purple shawl in order to feel sheltered and protected like the Indian women, and wished that she could be riding beside Tony. Maurice clung to the rail of the buggy seat and frowned as the ruts in the road threw them from side to side. Mabel enjoyed the mountains and the chasms and the birds that flew through the clear sky. "Every cell in my body," she records of their romance, "turned expectantly towards Tony" (191).

Had Mabel not considerable art in relating her tale of courtly love, her story would seem melodramatic. The note of sincerity which she conveys, however, makes one read with interest her descriptions of the Indian way of life and her love affair with Tony Luhan. On one occasion she carelessly dropped two little wild roses which Tony had picked for her. Her crest-fallen courtier picked them up and departed, but the hurt in his face remained with Mabel, so that twenty years later, she suffers in relating the incident, even though rejoicing that she learned about human love through it: "this small pain of his was more poignant to my unaccustomed heart than anything I had ever suffered. . . . the flooding into the blood of the realization of how another feels . . . was both terrible and desirable to me: terrible to know that until that instant I had been so insulated from others; desirable, oh, desirable, to come alive to them at last" (219).

The Indian way of looking at life changed Mabel. Although of course she built modern comfortable houses in Taos and could not herself have survived in the primitive living conditions of the Pueblo, still she did learn to appreciate the kind of unencumbered life in tune with the natural elements which Tony Luhan so thoroughly exemplified. His natural grace and ease among people, his perfect quiet, his lack of worry in situations that made the white men fret, all endeared him to the woman who was so ill-composed herself, so always striving for a way to happiness which he found in daily living.

Although they were not married until 1923, more than five years after they met, and then perhaps partly because of pressure from the Bureau of Indian Affairs, whose ward Tony Luhan was, their love for each other was genuine. *Edge of Taos Desert* is prefaced by a picture of Tony and includes a photograph of Mabel's left palm with its broken life line, meaning, she says, that the second half of her life unfolded with a new vision of wholeness. The story ends with Tony pitching his tent on Mabel's land, and after the departure of Maurice Sterne, asking:

"I comin' here to this tepee tonight," he said, "when darkness here. That be right?"
"Yes, Tony," I said, "that will be right."
And it was right.

Although Mabel lived another twenty-five years, she published no more volumes of her life's story. In *Edge of Taos Desert,* detailing the acquisition of a beautiful piece of land with Tony Luhan's advice, she perhaps explains why: "This earth and Tony were identical in my imagination and his, and I wanted to become a part of them, and the day the place became mine, it was as though I had been accepted by the universe. In that day I became centered and ceased the lonesome pilgrimage forever" (232). With the search for selfhood fulfilled, it would seem that she found no need to account for her life to herself or to others.[4] Mabel calls her life up to the time she came to Taos "years of amateur experience," of "nursery firesides," before she learned "what it really was to love and be loved, to suffer and to cause another to suffer" (233). Thereafter with Tony she experienced a mature acceptance of the ways of mankind and nature.

The Winter of Discontent
Made Summer: The Self at Ease

In spite of the important sales of her autobiographical volumes—created by the shock in Buffalo from the first volume of *Intimate Memories,* and the amusement or dismay according to whose character among the guests in Florence and in New York she portrayed in the next two volumes—Mabel's best written book went largely unnoticed. Two years before *Edge of Taos Desert,* she had written *Winter in*

Taos (1935) recounting a day in her life—a day in which, after Tony Luhan leaves for Arroyo Seco to trade oats for beans, she muses about his life and hers and about the changing seasons and the mythic return of spring after winter. Full of telling descriptions of the country around Taos, *Winter in Taos* has been compared to Thoreau's *Walden* in its deep feeling for the land and for man's place in nature. Whereas *Edge of Taos Desert* details may incidents relating to her break with Maurice Sterne and her becoming acquainted with the Pueblo Indians and their customs, as well as the visits of various guests to Taos, *Winter in Taos* is concerned with the very earth from which man gets his spiritual and physical sustenance. As such, it shows a maturity of thought and style beyond that of "amateur experience" or tales of "nursery firesides."

As she follows Tony Luhan in imagination after he leaves their own lane and the sound of the rattling Ford gradually recedes, she visualizes his passing Indian pastures and farmland, the little cemeteries with pale blue or white wooden crosses, the meadows so green and swampy in the summertime that munching cows are buried up to their bellies. Now the fields he passes are "blond with snow and pale, shining yellow grasses," while the sky above them is a cold, light blue. Beyond the fields, which are dotted with Indian horses, little adobe summer houses sleep during the winter "like forgotten rectangular boxes, with a bare tree or two hanging over each." At Placita, a little cluster of houses along Pueblo Creek, Tony passes over the bridge, while the creek continues on to Corierra and Cordóba, all small neighborhoods "that once had, each, their own little water mills where they ground the wheat between round millstones." Although Mabel regrets the passing of the old ways and the Indians' present practice of buying tasteless commercial bread, she admits to acquiring two of the old millstones for her own courtyard, while two more "of these ancient Taos stones lean against Jeffers's tower in Carmel."

In Placita, Tony passes the house of Spud Johnson, a friend of Witter Bynner's whom Mabel enticed to Taos as secretary and typist of her manuscripts, the editor as well of a local periodical, *Laughing Horse,* to which Mabel made contributions during the 1920s. The creek curves around his yard, in the middle of which is a sunken pool with flax and iris blooming around it in the summer, which he enjoys from his hammock between the trees. No mere summer visitor he, however, but warmed by a fireplace, with bookcases on each side in one small room, and a drum stove that burns all the time in the other, he is comfortable any night with "a fresh log snapping on the embers" and "the wild winter shut out." Without electricity but with the yellow light from oil lamps, Spud is happily in the care of those household gods who befriend the faithful, in contrast to the world's festivity seekers, who know little comfort in exciting distractions. In Spud's house every corner means something, intimate and special, with the kettle on the hearth and flowers abloom in the windows.

In Tony's passing further along the road, Mabel sees before her the places they have visited together—the cold ceremonial cave behind the waterfall, the fishing stream where Tony cooked beefstakes on a crotched stick, the little Mexican house where they were given hot chili, and the many picnic spots where they have ridden high up in the hills on horseback. Cantering home in the evening, "it is a race with the sun, sinking so fast over there; the western sky has a tumbled mass of clouds across it, all orange and violet and deep red edged with copper, and the Sacred Mountain, behind, is a flushed fiery rose for a moment. What privilege in the world is like this one, to move with this gayety through the sumptuous afterglow when the valley is all a warm bloom of light?"[5]

In reading this lovingly created book, one is carried along in imagination on Tony's journey into the mountains with his bag of oats, while Mabel, who is threatened with a cold, remains in her room, enjoying her thoughts of their life together. Time seems to pass like real time, as the reader too lives through the day. Even more magical, however, is Mabel's evocation of the four seasons in Taos and the country around the little town. Beginning with the cold winter day of the present, she remembers that spring will come, as always, then summer with its heat, autumn with its harvest, and once again winter with its snow. Describing every season with its virtues and its handicaps, Mabel creates a self at home in nature, all the philosophizing in this, her best book, being about man as creature of God's world. Absent is the mysticism, the psychiatry, the magic cures of scientism; present is the land of which Tony is a native part, the land that gives Mabel strength to be herself.

As her room grows colder in the late afternoon, her impatience with Boswell's *Life of Johnson* becomes so intense, that, reading among the travel-notes on France, "The moat of the Bastille is dry," she throws the book upon the floor. Fortunately for the reader, Mabel

begins to dream about the coming spring in vivid terms that are anything but dry. Remembering how sudden is its arrival after the
closed-in dark days of winter, she writes, "One evening, there is a
new light on earth. . . . The sky rises and is loosed in a vast, warm,
sighing heave. The village is bathed in a dark, tender gloaming that
is suffused with moist easiness, and the mountains that show at the
end of every road in this place . . . seem to breathe and stretch,
looming higher and higher" (W, 108–9). So Thoreau in the "Spring"
section of *Walden* writes: "It is seemingly instantaneous at last. Suddenly an influx of light filled my house, though the evening was at
hand." Instead of mountains Thoreau sees the water: "Where yester-
day was cold gray ice there lay the transparent pond already calm and
full of hope . . . as if it had intelligence with some remote horizon."
As he goes on to note man's spiritual rejuvenation in the spring, so
Mabel continues with a like reaction. As men cease to walk with their
heads bent in order to keep the heat within their collars, the light
that enlivens the dull earth shines in their eyes as well, and makes
everything—houses, horses, and even hearts—look larger in its warm
flood: "Everything likes each other, now, the sky leans tenderly to
the earth and the birds adore the sun, the fields begin to palpitate
and to steam, and green things prick and break through. The moist
manure has a delicate perfume that comes in the open window;
it suggests hyacinths and jonquils and one's heart opens to it"
(W, 112). Although the sap rises in the trees, the birds nest, and the
gardener feels little streams run down his back as he loosens the
earth, still another frost may nip and blacken the rising plants. During many a spring, Mabel writes, impatient to see the new daffodils
and narcissi, she has had the winter mulch removed, only to lose the
tender shoots. One is reminded of Robert Frost's woodchopper in
"Two Tramps in Mud Time," who on an April day, which seems like
May, suddenly finds himself in the middle of March. As a creator of
metaphor from nature, Mabel compares the development of friendship to that of a plant. "As in the growth of love and friendship,
when the flux and flow of relationship moves with its own momen-
tum too slowly, and one uncovers the roots in eagerness to reach the
flower, the bitter fruit of untimely haste and the arresting of love by
shock and an unseasoned hurry, are no more easy to endure because
the fault is one's own" (W, 117).

Having survived the false, when the real spring arrives Mabel sees
it as "the time when the world receives the light without the heat,

when the fire is high and does not consume, when the energy in every atom holds itself in equilibrium, unspilled, unbroken, and trembling in the balance" (*W*, 130). To her "The high potentiality of Nature reaches its zenith, now, before the months of overflow, and everything shines in continence, holding its own." Man must be wary of trying to hasten the growth which will burst forth in its own time during the summer. He may contemplate or adore, but not rifle the blossom: "Leave it to fall gently into fruition," she advises.

As her room darkens and the softly falling snow threatens blocked roads, the dreamer wishes Tony would come back. Her thoughts of spring, summer, and autumn now seem to bring not only the pleasures, but the discomforts of each. Summer, in spite of all its beauties, brings the heat that envelops the valley. After the early summer sweet briar rose, which has become "a pink froth all over the bushes that are thick in the lanes," the trees grow dark and heavy, "so thick their foliage, so umbrageous, they form an impassible wall at the west along the *acequia madre,* shutting out the sounds of the village and keeping the evening breezes off the house." The willow trees in the yard bend to the ground and "one must part the yellow-green and shining supple strands" to pass between them into the cool, shaded cavity formed by locust, cottonwood, wild plum, silver beach, and mountain elder intertwined to make "a transparent tapestry." Hollyhocks six and seven feet high and always alive with humming birds make a forest that one must wind through to reach the open fields beyond.

Avoiding the plaza of the town during the summer because of the many tourists, Mabel wanders through her apple orchard and her rows of peas, carrots, beans, squash, beets, and cauliflower. Sweet eating corn follows green peas as the peas succeeded asparagus. The cherry tree's fruit is harvested in "rows of canned cherries on the pantry shelves ready for pies and tarts." As she visualizes the dark shade beneath the plum tree bursting with ripe fruit, Mabel thinks how pleasant for her guests to breakfast in the open upon coffee and eggs and bacon, marmalade and toast, while they gaze from their shaded terrace at the "desert swimming in a blue haze" and across the miles of jade green stretches to the narrow opening out of the Rio Grande Canyon, . . . in the evening to lie in the hammock and watch the moon circle through the high branches of the cottonwood tree, its leaves motionless and black as thin iron." When one rides horseback in the summer, it is a relief, after the "humming heat in the long,

flat desert sagebrush," to enter the deep shade in the canyons and feel
the cool high air on one's face and on the sweaty horse (*W*, 157–58).

Summer is the time too when "color washes through everything
and surges up into all the fruits." The bright Indian paint brush
shoots out flames of fiery vermilion. Sometimes a clump of these scar-
let blossoms on a hilltop, swaying against the deep blue sky like a
beacon, fires the senses with the marvel of it. In the fields, waist-high
with oats, "long processions of slim, elegant turkeys mince in and
out of the stalks." Those returning to the valley from a summer
camping trip on the cold, treeless ridges of the mountains are surprised by the fields of wheat and corn, rich and luxurious, and by "a
thickness of living in the downy, sumptuous, golden valley" (*W*,
205).

As the evening wears on, Mabel's troubled thoughts envision the
slippery, narrow road back from Seco with Tony overturned in a ditch
and freezing to death with no help at hand. She reviews his good
work among the Indians, garnering support for self-government by
individual tribes, and his reports to John Collier, national Commissioner of Indian Affairs, whom Mabel had known in New York and
had persuaded to come west to help the Indians. In spite of her fears
and the cold night, she begins to reminisce about the season of autumn in her valley. "We feel how cool the evenings are and how early
the sun sets," she writes. The trees change color rapidly. "The sunshine seems yellower, and it blazes down in a full, walloping kind of
heat that is intense because of the cold edge already in the air." In all
the orchards the fruit is falling to the ground. Such an abundance of
red and white apples burdens her trees that she gives away many to
the Indians and to boys who come with empty sacks. "The air is
sweet with a fruity smell and the little pigs grow larger and run here
and there all over the place, eating as fast as they can" (*W*, 225).

By October the trees are fully turned and are "like torches of fiery
yellow, often with coral red tips, and others are big round balls of
radiant, sun-colored loveliness. . . . Day after day of Indian summer
passes, breathless," exclaims the admiring narrator, "when the whole
valley is immobile and every leaf is motionless, shining golden and
still. What days! One moves in a dream through the country, scarcely
able to believe one's eyes for the wonder of it" (*W*, 228). Now the
water in the ditches is full of yellow leaves, and the winds sweep in
blasts across the desert and buffet the walls. One must open the big
chests and take out the warm clothes, which smell of camphor and

must be hung out to air. The colts must be driven down from the uplands. The Indian women in the Pueblo are shucking ears of corn, with the husks piling up all around them. The ears, with all the sunset colors in them of pink, yellow, light red, crimson, and white, are hung out in long strings to dry.

But now the dreamer's thoughts come around again to winter and "the heart tightens up," not only because of the harsh coldness of that season but because of the lateness of the night with Tony still not home. So finally, driven into the center of her being, "into the most living kernel of us all," she finds relief. She knows that all is well. As the front door bangs shut, she runs to meet the traveler, expressing her fear that "something had happened" to him. His quiet reply of " 'What can happen?' " reassures her that in the world as he lives it, and in the natural pattern of the evolving seasons, indeed, nothing can happen.

Winter Reviewed

Critic Robert Van Gelder in the *New York Times* called *Winter in Taos* "a grandly ritualistic obeisance to the supremacy and rightness of the senses and the blood." With "mystic worship" he concludes, "nature and simplicity are brought very close, and there is something restful and healing about it."[6] Other critics responded in like vein. To one, although Mabel's prose was discursive, once accept "her leisurely backwards-forwards method of writing, and it becomes delightful."[7] Another remarked that "in many charming, slow-moving pages" Mabel Luhan makes it clear that Taos is a part of her and of that Southwest which she makes many an outsider long to know.[8] Still another remarked that even in unpolished prose "she can write, as she lives, with gusto," using an occasional fortunate phrase "beautiful in its ability to evoke an image."[9] Critics, having found nothing acerbic in the author's tone in this book, responded in kind with warm praise.

After writing *Winter in Taos* (1935) and *Edge of Taos Desert* (1937), Mabel, having portrayed her love for Tony Luhan and defined her relationship to the land of New Mexico, published no more of her life's story.

Chapter Five

Mabel and D. H. Lawrence:
Lorenzo in Taos

D. H. Lawrence in the New World

Of all her triumphs among the artists and personalities of her time, that of persuading British novelist D. H. Lawrence to come to Taos was undoubtedly Mabel's greatest. The story of the Lawrences' visit to New Mexico is related through letters and notes that they wrote to Mabel, and through her comments on the events of the time in the book *Lorenzo in Taos*. Published in 1932, it antedates even the earliest of her volumes of *Intimate Memories,* in none of which Lawrence is considered. That is, a separate volume, and her most popular, contains all her reconstruction of the experience of bringing this great British novelist to America and of the stormy times with him, with Frieda, and with their British friend, Dorothy Brett, who also came to live in Taos.

Having read in the *Dial* a chapter of *The Sea and Sardinia,* Lawrence's vivid account of living among the natives of the Italian islands of Sicily and Sardinia, Mabel *willed* him to come to Taos, being convinced that he could write as well about the Pueblo Indians. Not relying entirely on her psychic powers, however, she also encouraged him by the inducements of a home to live in and later the gift of a ranch twenty miles from Taos. At the time Mabel wrote them in the fall of 1921, Lawrence and his wife were still living in Sicily in somewhat temporary quarters; neither had been outside Europe. Mabel's extensive descriptions of the beauties of New Mexico and of the peaceful life of the Indians were tantalizing, and her assurance of comfortable living quarters was convincing. Hence both Lawrence and Frieda wrote that they would come as soon as passage could be arranged.

Mabel hastened to finish Tony's house for them, a five-room adobe thick-walled house close to hers, but on Indian land, with a stream running behind it, alfalfa fields in front, and facing the low hills and the Pueblo mountain. While the sun flooded the freshly whitewashed rooms, the portal between the two wings was cool, and the cottonwood trees furnished shade for the yard, fenced in by a low adobe wall. The ceilings were supported by heavy beams, glistening and smooth with the bark stripped off. The furniture constructed there by Indians and an adobe fireplace in each room gave the house an authentic look of being made by hands rather than machine. In Mabel's eyes it was nearly perfect.

All stood ready, even to the plants in the window, when Frieda wrote in January 1922: "We were coming *straight* to you at Taos, but now we are not. Lawrence says he can't face America *yet*—he doesn't feel strong enough! So we are first going to the East to Ceylon" (15).[1] And Lawrence wrote in the same vein, "I will come to the Indians, yes. But only via the East. There is something will not let me sail west for America." Since both urged Mabel to join *them* in Ceylon, whence all three could travel to Taos, Mabel suspected that they had been warned against her and wanted to meet her before proceeding to Taos.

Although in most of her story Mabel seems oblivious to what others think about her, here she admits that "it always hurt my feelings" to be criticized, but also it "stiffened my backbone" (16). Undaunted, therefore, she continued by letter to pursue the East-bound novelist, absolutely determined to bring him to Taos and most adamantly refusing to sail East herself. In June he wrote from Sydney that having found the disadvantages of the East, "It seems to me it is a good thing I came round the world to Taos. I shall be much more likely to stick it when I get there" (23). By the time they arrived in the fall, however, Mabel felt they had wasted nearly a year that would much better have been spent in Taos.

Not yet quite hardened to revealing her intimate life to the public, Mabel in *Lorenzo in Taos* used the ruse of writing to "Dear Jeffers," with the purpose of showing him "how we felt and acted some years ago." California poet Robinson Jeffers was another well-known literary figure whom Mabel enticed to Taos after the departure of the Lawrences. Always feeling that Jeffers and Lawrence should know each other, she had tried to encourage the relationship by sending to Lawrence two volumes of Jeffers's poetry, inscribed with a message from the Californian to the Britisher. Before the books reached him, Lawrence died in 1930 at the age of forty-five in Bandal, France, still writing Mabel in January of that year: "I believe I *should* get strong if I could get back: but I'm not well enough to travel yet" (350). Since the two men could never meet, Mabel, as the next best way to help Jeffers understand the novelist, wrote *Lorenzo in Taos* "to try and tell you about Lawrence."

Although in the book she reveals more about herself than about anyone else, she does admirably in explaining the difficult character of Lorenzo and his dependence on his German wife, Frieda. Mabel's was one of the early biographical accounts, and it has been a source of interest to students of Lawrence since that time. Further, the success of the volume encouraged Luhan's own development as a writer. Her first published book served as an impetus to its author to fill in her story up to that time.

The effect of New Mexico upon Lawrence, according to his own account, was tremendous. In comparing it to other places where he had traveled, he wrote: "I think New Mexico was the greatest experience from the outside world that I have ever had. It certainly changed me for ever. Curious as it may sound, it was New Mexico that liberated me from the present era of civilization, the great era of material and mechanical development."[2] None of his experiences in Ceylon or Sicily or Australia or Tahiti or California affected him as did New Mexico. "The moment I saw the brilliant, proud morning shine high up over the deserts of Santa Fe, something stood still in my soul," he exclaims. Although he appreciates the many kinds of beauty he has seen in other parts of the globe, "for a *greatness* of beauty I have never experienced anything like New Mexico." "It had a splendid silent terror, and a vast far-and-wide magnificence which made it way beyond mere aesthetic appreciation," Lawrence continues; it left one "stark, heartless, but undauntedly religious."

The religion of the Indians, Lawrence thought, was a cosmic religion, not "broken up into specific gods or saviours or systems," but preceeding god-religion and hence among the oldest known. He had had to travel the world to find a true religious feeling in the Red Race of New Mexico which he sensed nowhere else. His experience of the land and of the Indians revolutionized his mind and heart. It is somewhat paradoxical that Lawrence sought in America a new uncorrupted place to live, whereas the lost generation of American expatriates was at the same time seeking freedom in Europe.[3] But Lawrence was questing for a mythic regeneration from the old world's ills, whereas the young Americans fled the strictures of what they considered a Puritanical land of small minds. Lawrence found on the American continent in the native Indians the symbols of world regeneration which his quest eventually taught him must be integrated within oneself.[4]

Man's centrality and creative control of nature, suggested in Pueblo song and ritual, meant bringing "the mysterious and holy within the perspective of the human." The natural world fits man like a garment in an imaginative song of the Pueblos:

> O our Mother the Earth, O our Father the Sky,
> . . . .
>
> Then weave for us a garment of brightness:
> May the warp be the white light of morning,
> May the weft be the red light of evening,
> . . . .
>
> That we may walk fittingly where the grass is green.[5]

Just as Mabel was moved by the Indians' relaxed acceptance of the world and man's place in it, so was Lawrence impressed by the aboriginal faith which better taught how mankind should live than had the more artificial religions he saw practiced elsewhere.

Ups and Downs of the Novelist and His Patron

On the evening in September 1922, when the Lawrences finally arrived at the little railroad station of Lamy, twenty miles beyond Santa Fe, Mabel and Tony Luhan met them, each couple having had a tiring journey, one on the train from San Francisco, one over narrow, rutty roads from Taos. Their first supper together at the little lunch counter was not propitious; car trouble on the way to Santa Fe made it too late to obtain rooms; Mabel's thrusting the Lawrences upon Witter Bynner for the night was upsetting; all in all more angered words than pleasant passed among them that first evening. Next day, however, the rocky ride to Taos through the burgeoning September countryside was satisfying, and when after the final climb to Taos the Sacred Mountain came into view with its peaks forming a wide bow in the last red rays of the sun, "Lawrence and I knew each other through and through as though we were of one blood" (46). Never did she get to know him better than in those first few hours, though

Lawrence, like Tony, she admitted, was one of those rare people who could never be completely known.

First and last, Mabel's aim in getting Lawrence to Taos was to bring him together with the Indians. This aim was "like an impulse of the evolutionary will, apart from me, using me for its own purposes." During his three years in New and Old Mexico, however, she felt, in spite of one great novel, a novelette, short stories, and sketches, that he never portrayed the Indian spirit as she wished. Never ceasing to try to bring his vision to bear on the Indian culture, Mabel persuaded him to set out shortly after his arrival with Tony for the Apache Fiesta. A short piece he wrote was not very good, she surmises, because Frieda, through whom he felt everything, was not along on the trip. Its conclusion, "My way is my own, old red feather; I can't cluster at the drum anymore," denied the whole-hearted response to the Indian celebration which Mabel had hoped he would feel.[6]

Not averse, however, to his writing the novel about her life which he proposed, she tried to cooperate in this effort, which also did not bear fruit. Being an inexperienced writer, Mabel could only haltingly fill in the scenes which Lawrence asked her to amplify, especially in the overwhelming presence of Frieda. Thus the venture faltered, and instead Mabel appeared later in disguised form in other fiction of this great writer.

Socially the situation varied from day to day as it must with these four oddly grouped people—the slightly built, frequently acrimonious author; his large, earthy German wife; the wealthy Buffalo debutante, lover of a dark, broad-shouldered Indian; and the imperturable Indian, who worked long hours planting and harvesting his fields. At times hilarity reigned. Among the few social activities in which Lawrence felt comfortable was the acting out of charades, in which he let himself go quite unselfconsciously. Mabel is amused to remember Lawrence and Frieda being Tony and her in the front seat of the car. But the scene at which they all laughed was a representation of Mabel taking Tony to Buffalo to meet her mother, a scene which never took place in actuality as far as we know. Tony played himself, Ida Rauh played Mabel, and Lawrence, dressed in a huge hat and flourishing a lorgnette, played Mabel's mother, while other guests played various roles. Tony, wrapped in his blanket, very seriously making deep bows to Lorenzo, "was so funny we couldn't finish the act" (190).

The four took many excursions through the Indian lands and up and down the winding roads, sometimes by automobile, for Tony had become a very good driver, sometimes on horseback, after Mabel had taught the Lawrences to ride. Once they rode high up the side of the mountain to a rocky cave, which could only be reached by climbing on foot. The nearly obliterated trail led to the huge cavity, down the face of which plunged a waterfall, where Mabel on a former visit had had the mystical experience of forgetting her own tongue and being able to speak only in some arcane language. The Indians, fearing the bad spirits within, would not camp nearby, but the four intrepid climbers, skirting the waterfall, entered the cool, dark cavern to find a faint sun painted high on the wall facing the clear sheet of water across the opening. All felt together the magic of this ceremonial cave and its strange influences. Mabel later complained that Lawrence unjustifiably moved the sacrificial cave of his story "The Woman Who Rode Away" to the country of Mexico from its rightful place near Taos.

Many times they bathed in the hot spring, fifteen miles from Taos, which bubbled with life-giving heat from the earth's inner core. Undressing in the rock-walled shelter that Manby had built above it, each one descended slowly into the hot water, the women first, the men after. Mabel contrasts the human being, "keyed up, tightened beyond the normal pitch," with the same one who "sinks into the dark, grateful spring," and emerges with "the knots in the heart" untied. "You can imagine, Jeffers," Mabel addresses the poet, "how Lawrence loved this hot spring. He was at home with all natural, earthy things like that." Mabel herself was obviously affected: "The curious appearance of white bodies shining luminously, pale and green, in the mysterious water, the moist rock walls, one's swift response into an altered being in this real aqua viva—there was something primeval and archaic about it that took one back to other times" (181).

In addition to many other excursions and horseback rides, Mabel recalls, besides the charades, another happy occasion on the grounds of her big house. Two dozen Indians were sometimes invited to bring their feathers and bells, a big fire was built on the canopied hearth of the studio building, and moving in a circle to the exciting beat of a drum, everyone communally danced as one. "The air is filled with life and joy," according to Mabel, because with Indians life is not all

in the head but is diffused through their bodies. "They are forever
bathed entire in the flow and wash of it, so that their limbs have a
radiance, and an expression as vivid and speaking as a smile. Yes,
they talk, those brown bodies, and laugh" (193). Although Lawrence
abhorred the ballroom dancing which Frieda and Mabel and other
guests enjoyed in the evenings, he found irresistible the rhythm of
the Indians moving to the drum beat, and he danced "step, step,
with a dark one on either side of him, round and round in a swinging
circle for hours." No matter how restrained the whites at the beginning, Mabel writes, their blood is always wakened to the universal
pleasure of the bodies in motion together. "When anyone comes
within the radius of the vivid effluvium, the tissues know and react
to it," Mabel explains, and so they danced, becoming lighter and
happier by the hour. "At midnight everyone was joyous with lightened hearts" (194).

At another time Mabel and Lawrence sat together on the top of one
of the structures in Taos Pueblo to observe the ceremony of St. Ge-
ronimo's Day, when the wheat is garnered. Whatever Christian elements remain, the celebration is the Indians' own, with its pounding
race through the pueblo, the race that is not to win, but to give back
power to the earth which provides the harvest. Mabel's own involve-
ment in the rhythmic chanting made her believe that "Lawrence was
really in it. . . . It dissolved his painful isolation—breaking the barriers around him so that for a while he shared a communal effort and
lost himself in the group" (82). Lawrence did write a short essay,
"Taos," in which he described a ceremony in the Pueblo, hardly better than did Mabel herself, however, and with some added cynicism.
"It brings a sick sort of feeling over me, always, to get into the Indian vibration. Like breathing chlorine."[7] He nonetheless creates a
vivid picture of the brilliantly garbed Indians as they "trod the slow
bird-dance sideways, in feet of beaded moccasins, or yellow doeskin
moccasins, singing all the time like drumming coyotes."

In the fall of 1924, the two couples drove south to Navajo Indian
lands to see the Snake Dance in Hopiland, Mabel fervently hoping
that Lawrence would write and "tell all about that country before it
should die and become American" like the Buffalo, New York, which
she had left and like all the other towns and states. She believed that
Lawrence alone "could perceive and record the peculiar vestiges of another mode of life that have miraculously survived in the undisclosed
valleys of the Rio Grande River." Much to her disappointment, in

spite of a happy trip through the country with stops in Albuquerque and Gallup and sometimes in camps along the road, "he could not give himself to it." Lawrence's difficulty, Mabel surmises, is that "He never freed himself from his past or the past of his race. He recognized that life there was pristine, but he could not breathe for long in the rarefied air" (253). In any case, after writing what Mabel considered a dreary, day-by-day account of the long road to the Hopi village and of the dance, he later wrote a version, "The Hopi Snake Dance," of which she approved, along with an inspired description of the ceremonial at Santo Domingo Pueblo, "Dance of the Sprouting Corn."[8]

Interspersed with the periods of congeniality between Mabel and Lawrence and their spouses were many of sorrow and frustration, when pettiness, jealousy, and anger took over. Tony Luhan, of course, was his usual phlegmatic self, never angering Lawrence except when he laughed at the Britisher's first attempt at horseback riding. The friction between the two women, however, and that between Lawrence and each woman was often intense. Mabel exacerbated the tension between the Lawrences, first taking sides with the abused wife and then with the misunderstood husband, while Frieda, determined to thwart Mabel's will to power, tried to undermine her with Lorenzo. Mabel disavowed any interest in Lawrence physically, but in order to use him to create her Taos and its Indians through his literary imagination, she had to control him.

He, on the other hand, had ideas about women and work. Since he would have no servants in his house, he demanded that Mabel, too, scrub her own floor and bake her own bread. She made one lethargic attempt at the former, to the great amusement of her Indian servants, and one at the latter, the fruit of which Lawrence threw on the fire. He also had ideas about women's dress. Mabel, being somewhat "square," resembling she said not a willow but a pine of the Christmas tree variety, had always worn clothes that hung from the shoulder. When she hastened across the grounds to his house in a particularly pretty new flowing gown, he railed at Mother Hubbards and insisted she wear a belted dress, with a tight bodice and flowing skirt. To try to please, Mabel bought yards and yards of gingham and calico and had them made like Frieda's in the style he liked, under her breath denouncing this need of Lorenzo's "to be entirely surrounded by all sorts and sizes of persons dressed like his mother" (74). For awhile she even acquired and wore the aprons which he also considered part of a woman's garb. It was when he insisted on always being in the lead on horseback that she rebelled. She would race ahead, to be pursued by Lawrence, "pounding along as though his fate depended upon catching me." Perhaps they enjoyed the struggle between them, for to Lawrence "everything was significant and symbolic and became to him fateful in one way or another," making Mabel's life with him in Taos exciting and intense.

Perhaps Mabel should have known better than to ask Lawrence to give fatherly advise to her twenty-year-old-son John on the eve of his marriage to young Alice Henderson. She should perhaps have known what he would say: never let a wife know your thoughts. When she is gentle, be gentle, but when she opposes you, beat her. If the great black and blue bruises on Frieda's white body, which Mabel observed when they bathed in the hot spring, are any evidence, then Lawrence followed his own advice. The good days outweighed the bad, nevertheless, so Mabel grieved when Lawrence decided they should leave Tony's house and move to a rented ranch on Lobo Mountain after nearly three months as her guest. She thought her too great sympathy for Frieda had brought about the move, but whatever the cause, she went to Santa Fe on the day they moved "because I couldn't bear to see them go." Their cold thank-you notes left on the table in their main room shattered her. A month later when Lawrence wrote that they would like to visit her at Christmas time, she was still so hurt as to reply that her house was filled with other guests. Her pride would not allow her to welcome back the man who "made every least thing in life into something amusing and worth while" (101). The Lawrences left for Mexico, without a reconciliation. Later Mabel and Tony also left for a stay in Mill Valley near San Francisco.

In April 1924, however, the four returned to Taos, the Lawrences arriving at Mabel's big house with Dorothy Brett, who served, Lawrence once remarked, as buffer between him and Frieda. But Brett served only as annoyance to Mabel. She was a forty-year-old English woman who adoringly typed Lawrence's manuscripts and performed any services he asked. Besides being one more person always present with Lorenzo, Brett exasperated Mabel with her ungainly awkwardness and her large ear trumpet, which during social conversations she stuck in each speaker's face. Now Frieda was sometimes her ally against Brett. On one occasion, after trimming Lorenzo's beard, Mabel hoped that he would trim her hair, whereupon Brett instead seized the shears and started snipping away until she cut off the tip

of an ear of her astonished hostess, who, although she complained
heartily to Lawrence about the deed, had some admiration for its au-
dacious demonstration of hatred.

Soon the Lawrences moved to the ranch that Mabel gave them on
Lobo Mountain. Although letters passed between them from time to
time and Mabel and Tony visited the ranch, they did not, after one
frustrating experience ever stay overnight again in an adjoining cabin
that they had prepared for visits.

Whenever Mabel had a falling out with Lawrence, she writes, "I
had a queer relapse into psychic emptiness as though the bottom had
fallen out, and the queerest feeling of dispersal, as though my elements were 'just a pack of cards,' as in *Alice in Wonderland,* and Lorenzo had let them fall and scatter" (201). In words as well as in deeds
they flailed each other. Lawrence described Mabel to his German
mother-in-law: "very intelligent as a woman, another 'culture-
carrier,' likes to play the patroness, hates the white world and loves
the Indian out of hate, is very 'generous,' wants to be 'good' and is
very wicked, has a terrible will-to-power, you know—she wants to
be a witch and at the same time a Mary of Bethany at Jesus's feet."[9]
Mabel's view of Lawrence was that he was often cross or morose: "He
was all right so long as things went his way. That is, if nothing happened to slight him. He simply couldn't bear to have anyone question his power, his rightness, or even his appearance. . . . So, really
he was best off alone, with no one about to poke the hidden wound"
(82–83).

Reconciliation

How remarkable, therefore, that Mabel and D. H. Lawrence did
so much for each other. By the time Lawrence in 1925 wrote the
semifictional account of a man's return from the jungles of Mexico to
England, "The Flying Fish," he recognized that the deep ocean into
which the fish fall back is the reality of the life of the self, to which
it must always return. Changing scenes and frequent travels may
thrust the human being outside his native element, but home is
where he started from, the place to which he must return to face the
Great Reality of death which is the fate of all.[10] Besides the works of
fiction that he created in the new world, Lawrence learned to face his
human nature and to cease his ever-seeking journey toward a better
way, a new sensation, which was a flight from self.

Mabel, on her side, was inspired by Lawrence to write a number of poems which she includes in the volume. One, "False Start," in response to his letter advising that "Life put into you also the germ of something which still you are not," was published in *Poetry: A Magazine of Verse* in June 1926 and shows the influence of the Pueblos' attitude of living slowly in nature's rhythm.

Ask me no more of the full flower's speech,
Tell me no more of the ripe fruit's need,
For I am tired of trying to reach the fruit in the seed.

Leave me awhile, and I will recover
In darkness and night.
It was too soon for me to discover growth in the light.

Bear with my weakness, my failure, my pain,
Grant me this only, this darkness I need.
I sicken from sunlight, but give me the rain, for I am but seed.

Mabel felt that she could only write *for* someone and Lawrence was "positively the only audience I care to say something to" (276). She sent him chapter after chapter of her life story. In the spring of 1926 he wrote from Italy concerning the first book of *Intimate Memories.* "It's the most serious 'confession' that ever came out of America, and perhaps the most heart-destroying revelation of the American life-process that ever has or ever will be produced" (296). He sent her many suggestions on publishing, complimented her on the best sections, suggested ways of stirring her memory, and in general proved of great encouragement in her lengthy endeavor. "I do think the Memories extremely good," he wrote, suggesting that Aldous Huxley wanted to read them.

In a letter asking if she could provide any photographs for his book *Mornings in Mexico,* he wrote, "I'll dedicate the book to you, if you like: to Mabel Dodge Luhan, who called me to Taos." Later he repeated concerning the book, "They are essays I like. . . . I inscribed the book to you, as I said, since to you we really owe Taos and all that ensues from Taos" (324). Generous letters continued to pass between Mabel and both Lorenzo and Frieda, who also admired *Memories.* While in Florence in 1927, the Lawrences obligingly visited the Villa Curonia and sent on 218 volumes of what they decided were the best of Mabel's books, which Edwin, who still owned the villa, had not disposed of. After reading how Mabel as a girl loved colored ribbons in Buffalo, they also sent on a large selection of beautiful Florentine ribbons of all kinds. In turn Lawrence asked Mabel to distribute among her friends order blanks for *Lady Chatterly's Lover,* which he had had privately printed in an unexpurgated edition in Italy.

In their letters they forgot personal acrimony. In the last year of his life Lawrence wrote to Mabel, "If we can manage it, and I can come to New Mexico, then we can begin a new life, with real tenderness in it" (351). Forgotten was the chair she so lovingly constructed and upholstered for her guest, which he threw out with an unkind word; forgotten was the invaluable undesired gift of the manuscript copy of *Sons and Lovers* which Frieda gave Mabel in exchange for the ranch, and which she thought so lightly of as to give to Dr. Brill, her psychiatrist, in payment for helping one of her friends in New York. Forgotten were Lawrence's snubs of the company she invited to her house to help him get access to parts of Mexico; forgotten were his complaints that she tried to keep him too exclusively to herself. Forgotten were the battles with Brett and Frieda, both of whom came back to Taos to live after Lawrence died. There remained only an affectionate understanding of each other which apparently could not exist except across extended distances.

Mabel and the Critics

Some critics, in spite of making use of a great deal of Mabel's own analysis of her relationship with Lawrence, are exceedingly harsh in their judgment of her part in it. Christopher Lasch sees in her "a fatal susceptibility to intellectual quackery in all its forms." "Her letters to Lawrence, filled with intricate diagrams of psychic principles and with talk of introverts and extroverts, made him despair of her."[11] Although "the theme of sexual rivalry and hostility" was "the subject of practically everything she wrote," Lasch continues, "it was the favorite subject of Lawrence himself." Instead of concluding, however, that this gave them some affinity, Lasch judges that Lawrence wrote with "rare honesty," whereas Mabel's understanding of sexual conflict was only "half-articulated." Perhaps he unintentionally compliments her, however, in making any comparison at all of her with one of the greatest of twentieth-century writers.

Harry T. Moore in *The Intelligent Heart: The Story of D. H. Law-*

rence, finds nothing good at all to say about Mabel. From the first words concerning her relationship with Lawrence—"Taos was a mistake, as Lawrence realized soon after he arrived"—to his last grudging acknowledgment—"After his return to Europe they corresponded"—he critizes her motives, her actions, and her egotism. Perhaps he hardly realizes the humor in his apology: "The account of Lawrence's New Mexican experiences that follow will draw upon Mrs. Luhan's *Lorenzo in Taos* as little as possible."[12] The "little" proves to be quite a great deal and indicates that Mabel was at least partly accurate; *Lorenzo in Taos* would not have been quoted if it had been filled merely with sentimental sweetness or obvious falsehoods.

The account of some of the events in Taos by the young Danish painter who knew the Lawrences may be no more reliable than hers.[13] And perhaps the same can be said for Frieda's memories in *Not I, But the Wind* (1934). Of course the two women saw things differently, although Emily Hahn, in *Lorenzo: D. H. Lawrence and the Women Who Loved Him,* points out similarities: "They both believed that sex must be free and untrammeled. Frieda had taken Lawrence because she desired him just as Mabel had reached out and grabbed Tony."[14] Hahn's gossipy chapter on Mabel, "Wanted to Seduce his Spirit," draws heavily on Mabel's own account of her relationship to Lawrence. Where is the completely reliable recording of events? Not Witter Bynner's *Journey with Genius* (1951), which gives an unflattering picture of both Lawrence and Mabel. *Lawrence and Brett: A Friendship* (1933) by Dorothy Brett is bound to be a one-sided narration of the rivalry of Frieda, Mabel, and Brett for Lawrence's attention. Can one depend for objectivity on Lawrence's own letters, upon which so many critics rely for the facts? Are they not subject to distortion according to whom they were written?[15] If Mabel's are inaccurate, may not those of others be as well? Whatever the case, any critic of D. H. Lawrence must in some degree take account of Mabel's recording of the novelist's experience in America, which resulted in his creating, besides memorable critical and descriptive pieces, some excellent works of fiction.

Chapter Six
Mabel Dodge Luhan
in Fact and in Fiction

In The East

If Mabel may have given a distorted picture of others in her autobiographical volumes, the reverse is also true: others often supplied a distorted picture of her. Before and after she had published her own story, a number of her contemporaries portrayed her with only a modicum of truth or used her as the basis for the creation of a character not very similar to the real Mabel Luhan. Considering the great number of people to whom she was a personality, it is perhaps not strange that more than a few of them were inspired to portray her in fictional or semifictional form.

Besides the many guests at the Villa Curonia and the numerous participants in her evenings at 23 Fifth Avenue, many of whom also visited Finney Farm, she attracted writers, artists, and others to the cluster of houses in Taos, which Lawrence called Mabeltown. Besides Lawrence, Leo Stein, poet Witter Bynner, painter Andrew Dasburg, writer Mary Austin, and Indian Affairs Administrator John Collier, she played host to Thornton Wilder, Una and Robinson Jeffers, Elizabeth Duncan, Willa Cather, Robert Edmond Jones, writer Jean Toomer, Hollywood costumer Adrian, and artist Georgia O'Keeffe, and she corresponded with Eugene O'Neill, Scott Fitzgerald, H. L. Mencken, and Joseph Wood Krutch (who called her a "prophetess" and "a figure in recent cultural history").[1] With a touch of unintentional humor, a historical plaque recently placed at her graveside includes the information that, besides being an author herself, she was "an entertainer of numerous artists and authors." Although she would not have considered herself "an entertainer," she did perhaps amuse and amaze many an author and artist who portrayed her on canvas or in print. Since in Taos she purposely had a dining room table that would seat no more than eight, she did not entertain large crowds, but it was seldom that there were not a few guests in some of her houses, who took their evening meal at her large house, and who not infrequently described her in letters or in a fictional form.

Portrayals described in earlier chapters by those who knew her in Florence or New York include Gertrude Stein's "Portrait of Mabel Dodge at the Villa Curonia." When Mabel wrote an article on Stein's "Portrait" for the Armory Art Show, the editor commented: "This article is about the only woman in the world who has put the spirit of post-impressionism into prose, and written by the only woman in America who fully understands it,"[2] thus giving them both prominence during this important art exhibition. Mabel was only thinly disguised as a kind of mother-lover figure in two novels, as Edith Dale in Carl Van Vechten's *Peter Whiffle: His Life and Works,* and as Mary Kittridge in Max Eastman's *Venture.* Painted portraits include those of Jacques-Emile Blanche, Andrew Dasberg, and Maurice Sterne, and in sculpture that of Jo Davidson. Book reviews which humorously satirize Mabel are Cornelia Otis Skinner's "Dithers and Jitters," Malcolm Cowley's "Fable for Russian Children," and Clifton Fadiman's "The Making of a Squaw," subtitled, "Mabel Dodge and Tony (Red) Luhan in a passion-fraught story of two lovers who found each other in the wide-open spaces of the great southwest where men are men and women are memoirists."[3]

Interviews in the *New Yorker* upon her return visits to New York in 1940 and 1945 are hardly kinder. "Mabel's Tony" tends to present a ludicrous picture of a woman who, now over sixty, would presumably like to reestablish her salon in New York, but is tied to an Indian who wears a blanket, has never read any of her books or anything else in English, which he speaks haltingly, has never told her his Indian name, but has given her the Indian name of White Hawk, and who in New York "objects to having everything go on under roofs." In "The Chicken Pull" Mabel is made out to be a scatter-brained socialite who has just completed a novel called *Let's Get Away Together,* in which several returning service men end up in Taos at a chicken pull. The Indians have buried a chicken in the ground up to its head, which they try to pull off as they ride by on their speedy horses.[4] Strange that the *New Yorker* finds it worth while to interview so ridiculous a woman! Perhaps some of the harsh criticism of Mabel and her works resulted from the Eastern view that nothing artistically sophisticated could come out of the uncultured West.

Literary works for which Mabel furnished a model from her New York era include two by Neith Boyce and one by poet and playwright George O'Neil. Mabel was presumably the basis for the one-act play by Boyce called "Constancy," depicting in a somewhat humorous way the romance between Mabel and Jack Reed, the highs and lows of which the Hapgoods had been close observers. Neith Boyce also wrote a short story, "Retreat" (*Harper's,* December 1922), concerning a wealthy young woman's pursuit of a husband not her own, much to her mother's dismay. The sickly wife of the man, however, triumphs over the voracious female, who, like Mabel, has bobbed hair and wears flowing Florentine gowns.

George O'Neil, whose *American Dream* was produced on Broadway by the Theatre Guild in February 1933, may have used Mabel in his play as a model for the very disagreeable woman whose main occupation is giving cocktail parties for a decadent assortment of guests. The play shows the American dream as nightmare and the rich American woman as having no redeeming characteristics.

Besides the several portraits which he painted at the Villa Curonia, Jacques-Emile Blanche characterized Mabel in words in his autobiographical *Portraits of a Lifetime* (1938) and portrayed her as a character in his novel *Aymeris* (1923). In his introduction to his French translation of *Lorenzo in Taos,* he had stated that Mabel "passed over Italy like an aeroplane laden with explosives—I might add over all the earth." If one can read between the lines in Blanche's word portrait of Mabel, he may be most disturbed by her trying to persuade him, a traditional portrait painter, of the virtues of impressionism and later nonrepresentational schools. He admits, "Without making any show of the extent of her reading, she confounded me in argument. Her gentle but deep voice uttered things that disquieted me." In *Aymeris,* although the wealthy American woman who lives in Florence is named Giselle Links, her similarity to Mabel is unmistakable. George Aymeris, the young academic artist who comes to paint her portrait, learns about postimpressionistic art and the voracious nature of a domineering woman from her. Giselle exemplifies what Henry James so often portrayed, the confrontation of the brash American with the old cultures of Europe. Here that confrontation takes the form of the near-destruction of Aymeris, so ill-able to cope with a woman of such

strength of will and intellect, but it also portrays the dissolution of
the woman, who while mocking the decadence of the old partakes of
the decline of civilization through the orgiastic materialism of the
new.

In The West

Portrayals of the country around Taos and of Mabel, its chief pro-
pagandist, are many. The important woman novelist Willa Cather
spent some time in the early 1920s in one of Mabel's guest houses
and wrote parts of one of her best books, *Death Comes to the Archbishop,* while there. Although Mabel herself does not appear in the
novel, the character Eusabio seems directly based on Tony Luhan,
who had taken Cather to some remote and barely accessible Mexican
villages in the Cimarron Mountains. Eusabio is a Navajo Indian "extremely tall . . . with a face like a Roman general's of Republican
times. He . . . wore a blanket of the finest wool and design." Eusabio, like Tony, talks little, but has unfailing good manners and "a
contenance open and warm."[5] Mabel must be given credit for bringing Cather to Taos, and hence for the novel that emerged from her
experience of the land. Cather later highly praised Mabel's *Winter in
Taos,* calling it a lovely book of great charm, which reminded her of
the places she would like to visit again. No doubt Mabel is right that
in Cather's *Death Comes to the Archbishop* are also to be found "the ver-
ities she soaked up in Taos and Santa Fe, the little tales Tony told on
the long, slow, drives around the Valley in the summer afternoons,
and the simple immediacy of the Roman Catholic Church as it is
known here where its realities seem stronger than all its grand
organization."[6]

Another of Mabel's guests who was very fond of Tony Luhan was
the painter Georgia O'Keeffe, who spent one summer in the house
that the Lawrences had occupied. Tony took O'Keeffe to such places
as Mesa Verde, Inscription Rock, Canyon de Chelly, and the tiny village of Alcalde, near which she painted many desert and mountain
scenes. Like others of Mabel's guests, O'Keeffe had had to get some
miles away from too close proximity to her hostess after the first summer, but during the time she lived in "Mabeltown" she painted
scenes in the neighborhood of Taos, one of her best known being the
cross on the Mexican morada behind Mabel's big house. For many
years she had wanted to paint in the wonderful light of New Mexico,

which around Taos showed, she said, "a different kind of color from anything I'd ever seen"; but her marriage to Alfred Stieglitz had prevented her leaving New York, until in 1929 she was able to visit as Mabel's guest. Although she did not paint portraits of her hostess, she gave the world marvelous pictures of the Rio Grande Valley of northwestern New Mexico, fulfilling Mabel's aim of memorializing the land of New Mexico.[7]

Mary Austin, who came from the East to live in Santa Fe and whose best-known book, *The Land of Journey's Ending,* prophesies that the Indian culture of the Southwest may show the way for the rebirth of America, was a close friend of Mabel and Tony. She was aware that, before their marriage, considerable small-town opposition was growing to the relationship of Mabel and Tony Luhan and urged Mabel, whom she had also known in New York, to press for a divorce from Sterne and to make an allowance to Tony's wife, Candelaria. Austin recounts in her autobiography that automobile journeys of exploration with Mabel and Tony enriched her life. "Tony," she writes, "is an exceptionally good driver, not like the average American driver who constitutes himself merely the master of the car's mechanism, the exhibitionist, but making it the extension of his personality."[8] She testifies, like others, to Tony's singing the "accentless melodies of his people" as he drives, apparently adding another pleasant diversion to the long trips they took together. As a writer herself, she also testifies to the stimulating company of artists at Mabel's house in Taos, which she certainly contributed to, since she was as much in love with New Mexico and the Indian way of life as was Mabel.

Another friend whom Mabel had known in New York was John Collier, who visited her in Taos with his wife and three children and was there persuaded to take up the cause of the Pueblo Indians in their "struggle to save their lands, waters, and religions from Albert B. Fall's onset." Later he was made Indian commissioner in Secretary Harold Ickes's Department of the Interior, with Tony Luhan doing field work for him throughout New Mexico on behalf of the Indians. When Collier had attended Mabel's evenings in New York, he had discussed social problems of the city with some twenty guests, while Mabel herself, "a perfect and beautiful hostess, was always silent." In his memoirs, Collier refuses to try to characterize the woman who brought him into the service of the Indians, because so many have made the attempt, but "none have quite succeeded." Writing shortly after the deaths of Mabel and Tony, however, he pays them tribute.

"In their separate and their joined lives there has been beauty, generosity, naivete, human goodness, and a luminousness whose dying sundown gleam is around them still."[9]

Robert Edmond Jones, another admirer of Mabel, visited Taos after having a close friendship with her in New York and abroad. His theater designs were vastly influenced by New Mexican architecture, as Mabel notes in calling him "a seer" who "saw the life in the old handicrafts and in the ancient hand-built houses, where no spirit level was used, and no plumb line made straight mechanical forms one like another as off an assembly line. He saw the sensitive, refreshing shapes of which the eye would never tire. When he went back to New York he designed the settings for *Til Eulenspiegel,* performed at the Metropolitan Opera House, and they could have come out of Taos handmade."[10] An article which Mabel wrote for *Theatre Arts,* claiming that "A Bridge Between Cultures" might result from a recognition of the harmony between the Indians and the earth, is illustrated by a Jones sketch showing "A new temple in a new place."[11] This most prominent of theater designers was also influenced "by the leaning and irregular lines of adobe architecture, and the crooked crosses all askew" when, after his first visit to Taos, he designed the set for the *Macbeth* production in New York with Lionel Barrymore in the title role. The semiabstract construction made "audiences feel faint and ill" as they staggered from the theater.[12]

Thornton Wilder who had in New York at her behest, led a discussion elucidating *Finnegans Wake,* was another visitor who spent a number of apparently happy times with his sister Isabel in her big house in Taos. On the occasion of one visit Witter Bynner wrote a poem to Wilder, extolling the friendliness of New Mexico to the author-playwright, a response echoed by Mabel, who, as far as is known, never quarreled with Wilder, as she did with so many others. He made no secret of his admiration for her and thought highly enough of *Winter in Taos* as to be able to quote passages from it.

Leo Stein, who spent six months in Taos in 1917, considered Mabel "the all but perfect hostess," who had "the capacity to make things happen without any irritating restlessness" and who was the only cultivated person he knew to break "through the barrier between red and white."[13]

Other celebrities who came for brief or long periods included composer Igor Stravinsky, psychologist Carl Jung, educator John Dewey, and artists Marsden Hartley and John Marin. Novelist Thomas Wolfe arrived late one night, after Mabel had retired, and left the same night. Leopold Stokowski visited Mabel a number of times, out of interest in Indian music, which she hoped to have widely understood and appreciated. This musician, however, could not write down even phrases for lack of a scale, in spite of spending nightlong hours with unwearying patience in listening to the Indians sing. Another year he brought a recording device, but apparently deciding, like Mabel, that the spirit of the song could not be captured mechanically, he discarded the white man's invention in favor of the pleasure of unhampered listening.

Black poet and essayist Jean Toomer visited New Mexico in 1925 at Mabel's invitation to lecture on the mystic healer Gurdieff, in whom they were both interested. At one time Mabel considered housing a center for Gurdieff's followers on her land. Although Toomer did not stay long, he was later married in Taos and made contributions during the 1930s to the "New Mexico Writers" column of the *New Mexico Sentinel,* published in Albuquerque. A poem, "Imprint for Rio Grande," describes "that ether, the memory of earth above the Rio Grande, from Taos and above Taos" such that "I and everyone seem re-born upon that ark which still rides high, straight above the mesas of all sunken lands."[14] Toomer never equaled his earlier writing in *Cane,* but New Mexico spoke to him as it did to many whom Mabel brought to the state.

It cannot be said that Mabel's relationship with California poet Robinson Jeffers and his wife Una was any more peaceful than had been her association with Lawrence and Frieda. When the British couple left, Mabel, wanting a replacement who would be worthy to express the life of Taos, persuaded the reclusive Jeffers to visit Taos, to remain, she hoped, to become imbued with the spirit of the Indian life of the Pueblos. In spite of many visits, however, Jeffers was not inspired to write in Taos, his greatest contribution perhaps being as a listener, in Mabel's imagination, for *Lorenzo in Taos.* In giving chapters of the book to the poet as she wrote them, she did interest him and Una in Taos, where they visited annually through the 1930s.

Mabel must be given credit for perceptive reading of the best writers of her time. Owners of the bookstore in Taos testify that she bought books "in quantity, read them with lightning speed, and turned them over to the community library."[15] She felt in the misanthropic Jeffers, as she had in Lawrence, their sense of the end of a dying world and the search for a mythic new pattern to revivify man personally and socially. She herself had felt the ennui and boredom of a mechanized society of separated individuals, which, until her experience with the Pueblos, she had had no way of alleviating. Envisioning herself once more as able to persuade, cajole, and inspire a great artist, she wrote innumerable letters, recounting vivid stories of the life in Taos and the surrounding land, hoping to lure the poet from his retreat on the rocky coast of California.

That she succeeded may have been due partly to her flattery of Una and to a certain rapport between Mabel and the woman who arranged life for Jeffers as Frieda had for Lawrence. Both wives, although protective of their husbands against encroachment by Mabel or other women, had at the same time a close relationship with Mabel which excluded the husband. Though Jeffers found the visits taxing and could not work in the warm sunshine, he wrote to friends of the radiance of Taos Valley and of Luhan's *Winter in Taos,* "which describes it beautifully." In another letter he also paid tribute to Mabel's ability: "I don't see how Mabel Luhan manages to write so much so well."[16] Jeffers, nevertheless, did not respond to *Lorenzo in Taos* or to the land itself with any great epic or philosophical poem, but with Una continued their isolated life in Carmel. Thus Mabel suffered her greatest disappointment, blaming them both for failing in the expectations she had had of a poetry worthy of her land.

Witter Bynner, called in a recent review of his collected works "Prankster Poet," was a permament resident of Santa Fe when Mabel arrived. They naturally came to know each other very well and visited frequently, reading each other's work and enjoying common associates in the world of literature and art. Bynner's wit was such as not to be appreciated by everybody. Once it stung Mabel into a break in their friendship, which, similar to those she suffered with many other close friends, was healed in later years. In 1923 he had written a poem, "New Mexican Portrait of Mabel Sterne," which praised her as both an earth mother close to the life of the Pueblos, and a cultured lady who arranges life to suit her own tastes. She is a queenly figure of beauty with a shawl of "undulating flowers."[17] By 1925, however, with his friend Spud Johnson having left him to act as Mabel's secretary, Bynner felt strongly enough abused to write the farcical play, *Cake,* and to send Mabel a copy inscribed: "Cast your bread upon Witter and it shall return to you as Cake." Mabel apparently refused to read the play and certainly refused to attend the performance in

Taos in a filled auditorium, claiming that she did not want to steal the limelight from the author.

Bynner considered that "the slant of the play was sportive but not, I thought, malicious." He reports that Mabel was not amused but that D. H. Lawrence, when he received a copy in Florence, considered it "often very witty, and in parts really funny." Lawrence went on to add in his letter to Bynner, "I don't mind her passion for cake—it's her passion for breaking other people's eggs and making a mess instead of an omelette, which is really dangerous."[18] Bynner thought so too, apparently, in making Mabel an emasculating woman in search of her own satisfaction, regardless of the discomfort of others. Whatever Mabel's reaction to the play, she probably enjoyed the publicity and the ongoing battles with Bynner. She had written a poem for Bynner and Johnson's *Laughing Horse* magazine called "Ballad of a Bad Girl"[19] in which the bad girl goes to Heaven where "Honey-cake and ether was a sweet, sweet fare." Although not the wit that Bynner was, Mabel may be making fun in this poem, which was accompanied by an illustration by Lawrence, of the men who think a girl should be a wife and mother rather than an aspirant for the heights which only men can reach. The play *Cake: An Indulgence* (1926), fancifully portrays a lady as emasculator of men, symbolized by her servants, a unicorn, carrying his horn in his hand. Bynner was indeed a prankster, having in 1916 written a lampoon of the imagists and vorticists which was taken seriously, and in 1935 in *Guest Book* having caricatured many guests in individual sonnets, Mabel for one in "Gourmande." *Cake* was "an indulgence" on Bynner's part to engage in satire of Mabel, as it was "an indulgence" on hers to want to eat cake and have it too.

Myron Brinig, an American novelist of the 1930s who wrote about the Midwest, first visited Mabel in 1934. Thus he came to know her later than others who used her in their fiction or drama or essays, his book *All of Their Lives* (1941) being based partly on her own autobiographical volumes, all of which had appeared by 1937. Brinig's portrait lacks the humor of Bynner's, one reviewer comparing the heroine to Becky Sharp in *Vanity Fair,* who goes her own selfish way, disregarding the feelings and welfare of others.[20]

Brinig shows Florence Gresham as coming out of a Victorian background and hence subject to its mores, at the same time freeing herself from many of its restrictions, but not without a sense of guilt. Prohibited from many pursuits by her sex, she achieves importance by making numerous males subject to her will. Thus Brinig and other men who characterized Mabel see her as failing in the traditional role of wife and mother, and instead gaining satisfaction at the expense of the male. Brinig finally finishes off his heroine in the West: racing ahead on her plunging horse, she is consumed, along with her horse, by a bolt of lightning. Brinig seems, like Lawrence, to endow Mabel with the mythic quality of one in the care of the gods. In the end life seems to have been enriched by the existence and sacrificial death of Florence.

In the Fiction of D. H. Lawrence

Although the novel which Lawrence planned to write about Mabel's life never materialized, she nevertheless appears in disguised form in two short stories, "None of That" and "The Princess," in two longer stories, "St. Mawr" and "The Woman Who Rode Away," in the novel, *The Plumed Serpent,* and very indirectly in his impressionistic survey, *Studies in Classic American Literature.*

In "None of That" Ethel Cone, a rich American woman in Mexico, who will have "none of that" sexual foolishness with the men of her acquaintance, becomes entranced with a daring bullfighter, Cuesta. In reality despising her, he invites her to his home in a poor part of the city, where he has her raped by half a dozen of his bull ring gang. Since the urges of her body have overcome her imagination, she kills herself after bequeathing Cuesta half her fortune. A disagreeable story, it takes a terrible male revenge on the type of American woman who tantalizes men while holding herself aloof. To reinforce the theme, the story is narrated by a man whom she treats coldly but who, having lost his money, must serve as her escort. Since Ethel Cone has a number of features similar to Mabel's, it would seem that, if Lawrence could not finish her off in fact, he could do so violently in this piece of fiction.

The princess, in the story of the same name, is Dollie Urquhart, daughter of widowed, slightly mad Colin Urquhart, who has taught her continuously through their very close and isolated association that she is superior to all other people, whom she must nevertheless treat with cold politeness. After his death she goes with a female companion to a ranch in New Mexico, where she allows a Mexican guide to take her on an expedition into the mountains. Her cold contempt for his lovemaking, which she had encouraged, angers him to the point of making her stay with him until she is rescued by forest rangers. Thereafter she is always slightly mad. Once more Lawrence shows scant sympathy for the superior acting rich woman whose blood is cold to human relationships. The horseback riding through mountain trails comes from Lawrence's own experiences with Mabel in Taos, as does his view of her inability to give herself to love. The ego-fostered will, which makes such an American woman inhuman, he suggests, should be sublimated to the natural forces of a love that brings a man and woman together in harmony.

In "The Woman Who Rode Away," set in Mexico, but closely resembling the scenery near Taos, with its cave behind the waterfall, "the woman" resembles Mabel in lacking a purpose in life. Although the story might seem similar to the former two, it proves vastly different in tone and theme. Abandoning her husband, who owns nearby silver mines and ranches, and her two children, she rides alone into the wild mountains, inhabited by a tribe of Indians who hold her captive and sacrifice her on the altar in the cave to their Sun God. The woman participates willingly in the mythic sacrifice, which gives meaning to her formerly useless existence. In an era of woman's liberation, the story has proved subject to different interpretations by Normal Mailer *(The Prisoner of Sex)* and Kate Millett *(Sexual Politics)*.[21] In reality the woman fulfills the prophecy that when a white woman gives up the whites' God and submits to the God of the Indians, the world will be reborn. The story, rather than being a tale of horror or an expression of male dominance over a drugged female victim, expresses Lawrence's hope for America that a new faith may vitalize the earth. Although Mabel may not closely resemble the woman, it was she who took Lawrence to the magic cave and who had had the courage to cast off the effete life of the urban East in favor of the simple life of Taos. It can hardly be doubted that her life gave him the idea for his character, and that he compliments her in its creation.

In "St. Mawr" Tony Luhan is characterized as Phoenix, a Navajo Indian, who is serving in England as a horse groom for a Mrs. Witt and her daughter, Lady Carrington, and who accompanies them on rides in the London parks and in the English countryside, riding "as if he and the horse were all one piece." He is delighted when they decide to return to America to buy a ranch very much like the Lawrences' on Mt. Lobo. Lawrence obviously bases his descriptions of the New Mexican deserts and mountains on his experiences in Taos and his two women characters on various aspects of Mabel Luhan. Mrs. Witt, who tries to dominate her daughter and son-in-law, and Lou, who forces her unwilling husband to try to ride the excitable stallion St. Mawr, are characterized as the kind of women who end up searching for a happiness they never find, even in the natural beauty of the Southwest. Both women, too world-weary to be able to give themselves to love, look down on men as dishonest sensation-seekers. Whereas Phoenix is at peace with himself and the universe, the women, although rich, are at odds with themselves and their surroundings.

Although Lawrence's somewhat unformed stories leave the resolution inconclusive, in this case Mabel and Tony certainly furnished models for the mother, daughter, and Indian groom, and Lawrence's learning to ride in New Mexico provides his vivid portrayal of the nervous, powerful St. Mawr, threatened with emasculation, but a creature not to be controlled by mere force. In spite of Lou's feeling that the ranch she has bought is beautiful enough to be "bigger than men, bigger than people, bigger than religion," "something to do with wild America," a certain irony lies in its name, Las Chivas, for "the goats" have denuded the land. Lawrence thus again expresses his paradoxical feelings about Mabel and about America. Since the Phoenix bird, which resurrects itself from its own ashes, was a symbol of special significance to Lawrence, he would seem to compliment the Indian groom by naming him Phoenix.

In *The Plumed Serpent* a forty-year-old, Mabel-like character, Kate Leslie, bereft by the death of her Irish revolutionary husband, visits Mexico with an American cousin, lifelessly not caring what the future may bring. Something compels her to remain alone in a remote area of the country in a lakeside house which is near the residence of Don Ramon Carrasco, who is leading the movement of the people back to the old God Quetzalcoatl. Jesus has outlived his time in Mexico, is now the old God, and must depart. Kate goes through the mythical process of descending into despair and then rising in hope through her love for Don Cipriano, the chief follower of Don Ramon, and of assisting in the resurrection of a degenerate people through Ramon as representative of the God Quetzalcoatl.

As in "The Woman Who Rode Away," in which a white woman who submits to the faith of the natives finds her own soul in the process, so Kate is reborn, somewhat as Mabel through writing her four volumes of self-analysis reached a level of peace after much seeking and many travels here and abroad. According to L. D. Clark in *The Dark Night of the Body: D. H. Lawrence's "The Plumed Serpent,"* "the theme of the woman in search" Lawrence made "the dominant one in every important piece of fiction that he wrote from the inspiration of this continent," and most of his American heroines "possess traits of character drawn from Mabel Luhan and had experiences suggested by the events of her life. Her affair with Indian Tony Luhan and their eventual marriage furnished Lawrence with a starting point from which to develop the white lady–dark lover situation between Kate and Cipriano."[22] It may also be true, as Witter Bynner suggested to Lawrence, that Mabel's interest in various kinds of mysticism led to development of the Quetzalcoatl theme of the novel.

Mabel can hardly be said to have influenced Lawrence's views of Cooper, Hawthorne, or Melville in his collection of opinionated essays, *Studies in Classic American Literature.* Perhaps, however, such a remark as "White Americans do try hard to intellectualize themselves. Especially white women Americans," is a result of his knowing Mabel, as is "Supposing an Indian loves a white woman and lives with her," still there is "no reconciliation in the flesh" between races. More importantly, in his introductory chapter, "The Spirit of Place," he senses something of what Mabel hoped he would in the new land of America among people of various races, moving through a "false dawn" toward true understanding of self.

In Fact

If Mabel had done nothing except to furnish the model for five important pieces of fiction of one of Britain's greatest novelists, she would have been worthy of more than a footnote in the history of literature. As it is, besides the many others she inspired to characterize her, she did far more as a competent writer who herself provided American letters of the twentieth century an interesting record of a unique personality and of the several cultures in which she lived during the first decades of the century. Whereas some read her books hoping to pick up bits of gossip, serious critics soon became aware of the clear eye of their author, the frequent felicitous phrase, and above all the honest self-appraisal whereby she elucidated her life and the life of her times. Critic Elizabeth Shepley Sergeant, calling her "Sphinx of Taos Desert," says that it is "really too bad" that the public has come to read her works for their scandal content, "rather than

for their real literary merit, their re-creation of the past, their portraits, burning narratives, and visual perceptions." Calling her at the
end of the 1930s "the most talked-about woman in the Southwest,"
Sergeant enumerates, besides other friends, certain of "the artistic
confraternity, who are wise enough to recognize in Mabel Luhan a
sort of genius at the mercy herself of the play of negative and positive
forces with which all artists have to reckon."[23] That so well-known a
critic as Sergeant, who knew Mabel personally, calls her, in spite of
pettiness, "a sort of genius" is testimony to Mabel's artistic accom-
plishment as a writer.

Although she wrote innumerable letters and private accounts of
various events throughout her life, her work in the main consists of
the six books published in the years between 1932 and 1937. Her
first, *Lorenzo in Taos* (1932), although lacking in the form which the
four volumes of *Intimate Memories* have by virtue of their chronological
order, coheres as a work of art through its concentration on the relationship of Mabel and Lawrence. Her commentaries on his many letters make the personalities of both come alive, and as one critic
noted, great pleasure also arises "from the picture of the New Mexico
which Mrs. Luhan knows so thoroughly, sees so accurately and feels
so poignantly."[24] Another concluded, "*Lorenzo in Taos* is one of the
most interesting literary portraits ever to be published, not alone for
what it reveals about its subject but for what it reveals about the artist who did the portrait."[25]

In the four years between 1933 and 1937 Mabel completed the
four volumes of *Intimate Memories,* a title perhaps offensive in itself to
that social set in Buffalo where she grew up, but foretelling a new
age of frankness in twentieth-century life and art. Moving from the
first volume, *Background,* to *European Experiences,* with its details of
her life in Florence, Rome, Paris, and other foreign cities, she wrote
her largest volume, *Movers and Shakers,* in 1936, dedicating the first
part to her lover "Jack Reed the Poet" and portraying her grand passion in terms which spared neither herself nor him.[26] A reviewer
called the author "at once high-strung and imperturbable, gushy but
shrewd, a celebrity-hunter, falling for all manner of artistic fakers but
preserving a strong streak of hard-headed commonsense."[27] When she
came to the fourth volume with its picture of blanketed Tony Luhan
as frontispiece, her tone was not that of "frozen-faced malice," but of
awe before the quiet emptiness of the desert on whose edge the In-

dians lived in harmony with nature. *Edge of Taos Desert* was said to show "the fervor, the certainty and the mysticism of the recent convert."[28]

For literary merit none of the four volumes of *Intimate Memories* surpasses or perhaps even equals *Winter in Taos,* the simple story of a day in the life of a woman who loves her husband and who imagines as the day passes that the seasons of the year too pass in a never-ending cycle which encloses the pair. In the midst of writing her autobiography Mabel paused in 1935 to create this heartfelt idyll, a paen to love and nature.

After 1937 Mabel wrote only short articles or poems which were published in periodicals, until in 1947 she compiled a volume, *Taos and Its Artists,* consisting of short biographies and reproductions of the paintings of nearly fifty artists. Although she was no doubt well qualified to select the artists and note some biographical details of their lives and work, the book is of more interest as evidence of the growing art colony in Taos than as literature.

The six books described, however, can hold their own in the world of letters. Even though slightly malicious and lacking a sense of humor at times, Mabel was honest enough to see her own faults and assume the blame for her own dissatisfaction with life. As something of a celebrity before she had written any books, she was the subject of caricature in the works of several writers. Although she never forgave Harvey Fergusson for his satire of Tony Luhan in *Footloose McGarnigal,* she bore criticism of herself with fortitude.[29] When she came to write her own memoirs, she drew an accurate picture of her life and times. Mabel herself and her autobiographical volumes are thus remarkable products of the early decades of twentieth-century America.

Just how valuable was her contribution as a recorder of the era may not be known until Yale University makes her papers available for study. According to curator Donald Gallup, the holdings include, besides innumerable letters written by her and to her, the manuscripts of a number of extensive autobiographical accounts from various periods of her life, two full-length novels, three scenarios, a number of short stories, essays, and poems. Although this unpublished material will not be available for some time, Gallup concludes, "The complete autobiography when it can eventually be used by scholars will constitute an invaluable record of the period as seen by a woman of a superior order of intelligence and understanding, gifted with an extraordinary memory and a natural talent for self-expression."[30] Before the end of the century, therefore, even more light may be thrown on its early years by the work of Mabel Luhan, who published only part of what she recorded for the future about herself and her times.

Notes and References

Chapter One

1. Quotations followed by page numbers in this chapter are from *Intimate Memories: Background* (New York, 1933).
2. *Forum* 89 (May 1933):v.
3. *London Times Literary Supplement*, 12 October 1933, 694.
4. *New York Evening Post*, 18 March 1933, 7.
5. *Books*, 19 March 1933, 3.
6. *New York Times*, 26 March 1933, 4.

Chapter Two

1. Quotations followed by page numbers in this chapter refer to *European Experiences* (New York, 1935).
2. Emily Hahn, *Mabel: A Biography of Mabel Dodge Luhan* (Boston, 1977), 23. Hahn's book contains no annotations or footnotes and only a brief bibliographical note on some dozen volumes from which Hahn gathered documentation. She did, however, confer with Luhan's one-time daughter-in-law Alice Henderson, who had married John Evans in Taos. She also consulted unpublished material by Luhan on deposit in the Yale University's Beinecke Rare Book and Manuscript collection. Thus unpublished and undocumented sources enable her to make reasonably accurate judgments.
3. See Christopher Lasch, *The New Radicalism in America 1889–1963: The Intellectual as a Social Type* (New York, 1965), 107; and Patricia Spachs, *The Female Imagination* (New York, 1975), 218.
4. Gertrude Stein, "Three Painters," in *Selected Writings,* ed. Carl Van Vechten (New York, 1962), 334.
5. Comments which Alice later wrote about Mabel are no more flattering than was Mabel's characterization of her. In *Collected Letters of Alice B. Toklas,* ed. Edward Burns (New York, 1973), 92, she writes that Mabel was "just the same repetition with nothing added or taken away and she was deadly dull. But she did have a pretty old-fashioned coquetry." In *What is Remembered* (New York, 1963), 76–77, Alice acidly describes a scene at the villa where after dinner Mabel, "stretched out on one of the long sofas," was talking intimately with Andre Gide, who, "sitting opposite, was leaning over her," both oblivious to the amusement of the other guests.
6. Stein, *Selected Writings,* 529.
7. *The Flowers of Friendship: Letters Written to Gertrude Stein,* ed. Donald Gallup (New York, 1953), 72.

8. Mabel so badly offended Gordon Craig by belittling their plan that he later refused to see the young designer, Robert Edmond Jones, for whom she sent Craig a letter of introduction. See Orville K. Larson, "Robert Edmond Jones, Gordon Craig, and Mabel Dodge," *Theatre Research International* 3 (February 1978):125–33.

9. See Foreword to *The Letters of Ruth Draper, 1920–1956,* ed. Neilla Warren (New York, 1978).

10. D. L. M. in the *Boston Transcript,* 2 November 1935, 4.

11. See chapter 14, "In Italy with Mabel Dodge," in Jo Davidson's *Between Sittings: An Informal Autobiography* (New York, 1951), 82.

12. This and the immediately following quotations from Rubinstein appear in *My Young Years* (New York, 1973), 414–15.

13. Cornelia Otis Skinner, *Dithers and Jitters* (New York, 1939), 4–5. The title is a take-off on Mabel's volume *Movers and Shakers.*

14. Mina Curtis in the *Nation* 141 (27 November 1935):628.

15. Muriel Draper, *Music at Midnight* (New York, 1929).

16. W. G. Rogers, *Ladies Bountiful* (New York, 1968).

17. *Chicago Daily Tribune,* 21 September 1935, 14.

18. *New York Herald Tribune,* 20 September 1935, 13.

19. *Books,* 22 September 1935, 9.

20. *Nation* 141 (27 November 1935):629.

Chapter Three

1. Quotations followed by page numbers in this chapter refer to *Movers and Shakers* (New York, 1936).

2. *Saturday Review of Literature* 15 (21 November 1936):7.

3. Hutchins Hapgood, *A Victorian in the Modern World* (New York, 1939), 275.

4. Ibid., 287

5. Ibid., 410.

6. Ben Ray Redman, *Edwin Arlington Robinson* (New York, 1926), 20.

7. Linda Simon, *The Biography of Alice B. Toklas* (Garden City, N.Y., 1977), 278.

8. *Selected Letters of Edwin Arlington Robinson,* ed. Ridgely Torrence (New York, 1940), 115.

9. Edward Lueders, *Carl Van Vechten* (New York, 1965), 26.

10. Carl Van Vechten, "Some 'Literary Ladies' I have Known," *Yale University Library Gazette* 26 (January 1952):105.

11. Stein, *Selected Writings,* vii.

12. Carl Von Vechten, *Peter Whiffle* (New York, 1922), 119.

13. Ibid., 124.

14. Lueders, *Carl Van Vechten,* 29.

15. The collection contains, among hundreds of others, 60 letters from Robinson, 183 from Van Vechten, and 278 from Neith and Hutchins Hapgood. See Donald Gallup, "The Mabel Dodge Luhan Papers," *Yale University Library Gazette* 37, no. 3 (January 1963):97–105.

16. Hermann Hagedorn, *Edwin Arlington Robinson: A Biography* (New York, 1938), 281.

17. Richard O'Connor and Dale L. Walker, *The Lost Revolutionary* (New York, 1967), 70–90.

18. Allen Churchill, *The Improper Bohemians* (New York, 1959), 133–34.

19. Malcolm Cowley, *New Republic* 89 (25 November 1936):120–22; reprinted in *Think Back on Us: A Contemporary Chronicle of the 1930's* (Carbondale, Ill., 1967), 123–26.

20. Churchill, *Improper Bohemians,* 89.

21. Max Eastman, *Love and Revolution* (New York, 1959), 6.

22. Max Eastman, *Enjoyment of Living* (New York, 1948), 523.

23. Max Eastman, *Venture* (New York, 1927), 63.

24. Ibid., 206.

25. Ibid., 24.

26. Ibid., 25.

27. Milton Cantor, *Max Eastman* (New York, 1970), 33.

28. William O'Neill, *The Last Romantic: A Life of Max Eastman* (New York, 1978), 29.

29. "Fiftieth Anniversary of the Famous Armory Show," *Art in America* 51 (February 1963):31–37.

30. Bruce Kellner, *Carl Van Vechten and the Irreverent Decades* (Norman, Okla., 1968), 68.

31. Waldo Frank et al., *America and Alfred Stieglitz: A Collective Portrait* (New York, 1975), 112.

32. W. G. Rogers, *Ladies Bountiful* (New York, 1968), 120.

33. Victor Seroff, *The Real Isadora* (New York, 1971), 216.

34. *Shadow and Light: The Life, Friends and Opinions of Maurice Sterne,* ed. Charles Meyerson (New York, 1965), 121, 146–47.

35. *Women's Autobiography,* ed. Estelle C. Jelinek (Bloomington, Ind., 1980), 163.

36. See Richard Hofstatter, *Anti-Intellectualism in American Life* (New York, 1963), 205; Justin Kaplan, *Lincoln Steffens* (New York, 1974) 199; and Alfred Kazin, *On Native Grounds* (New York, 1942), 167.

37. See Lois Palken Rudnick, "The Unexpurgated Self: A Critical Biography of Mabel Dodge Luhan" (Ph.D. diss., Brown University, 1977), 172–74.

38. Patrick F. Palermo, *Lincoln Steffens* (New York, 1978), 83.

39. Oscar Cargill, *Intellectual America: Ideas on the March* (New York, 1941), 507.

40. Peter Minuit, "291 Fifth Avenue," *Seven Arts* 1 (November 1916):64.

41. Euphemia Van Rensselaer Wyatt, "For the Waste-basket," *Commonweal* 25 (11 December 1936):199.

Chapter Four

1. *Taos and Its Artists* (New York, 1947), 11.

2. Quotations followed by page numbers in this chapter refer to *Edge of Taos Desert* (New York, 1937).

3. Ruth Benedict, *Patterns of Culture* (New York, 1934), 128–29.

4. Mabel Luhan's later works were objective. *Taos and Its Artists* reproduces the paintings of artists of Taos with short commentaries on their lives and work. She edited an issue of the *New Mexico Quarterly* (21 [Summer 1951]) which dealt with "Taos and Individualism" and included her essay, "Paso por Aqui!" (137–46), detailing the stories of various artists and writers who were inspired by Taos. In "Holiday from Science?" *Southwest Review* 31 (Summer 1946):221–24, after describing the beauties of Taos and the Indian life, she wonders if the atomic scientists working nearby, "Up on The Hill down the river," will destroy it all.

5. *Winter in Taos* (New York, 1935), 186; hereafter cited below as *W*.

6. *New York Times,* 7 April 1935, 2.

7. D. L. M. in the *Boston Transcript,* 4 May 1935, 6.

8. *Nation* 140 (1 May 1935):516.

9. A. K. Parker in *Commonweal* 22 (17 May 1935):82.

Chapter Five

1. Quotations followed by page numbers in this chapter refer to *Lorenzo in Taos* (New York, 1932).

2. "New Mexico," in *Phoenix: The Posthumous Papers of D. H. Lawrence,* ed. Edward D. McDonald (London, 1961), 142.

3. Armin Arnold, *D. H. Lawrence and America* (London, 1958), 129.

4. James C. Cowan, *D. H. Lawrence's American Journey: A Study in Myth and Literature* (Cleveland, 1970).

5. Franchot Ballinger, "The Responsible Center: Man and Nature in Pueblo and Navajo Ritual Songs and Prayers," *American Quarterly* 30 (Spring 1978):102.

6. The entire essay appears as "Indians and an Englishman," in *Phoenix,* ed. McDonald, 92–99.

7. Ibid., 101.

8. D. H. Lawrence, *Mornings in Mexico* (London, 1965), 54–80.

9. Frieda Lawrence, *Not I, But the Wind* (New York, 1934), 159.

10. *Phoenix*, ed. McDonald, 780–98.

11. Lasch, *The New Radicalism in America*, 124.

12. Harry T. Moore, *The Intelligent Heart* (New York, 1954), 297.

13. Knud Merrild, *With D. H. Lawrence in New Mexico* (London, 1938).

14. Emily Hahn, *Lorenzo* (New York, 1975), 238.

15. Editions of Lawrence's letters are *The Collected Letters of D. H. Lawrence*, ed. Harry T. Moore (London, 1962), and *The Selected Letters of D. H. Lawrence*, ed. Diana Trilling (New York, 1958).

Chapter Six

1. Joseph Wood Krutch, *More Lives Than One* (New York, 1962), 217.

2. John Malcolm Brinnin, *The Third Rose: Gertrude Stein and Her World* (Boston, 1959), 185.

3. *New Yorker* 13 (18 September 1937):72–73.

4. "Mabel's Tony," *New Yorker* 15 (3 February 1940):14–15; "The Chicken Pull," *New Yorker* 21 (5 May 1945):17–18.

5. Edward A. Bloom and Lillian D. Bloom, *Willa Cather's Gift of Sympathy* (Carbondale, Ill., 1965), 206.

6. "Paso por Aqui!" *New Mexico Quarterly Review* 21 (Summer 1951):139.

7. "Profiles: Georgia O'Keeffe," *New Yorker* 50 (4 March 1974):53–56.

8. Mary Austin, *Earth Horizon: An Autobiography* (Cambridge, Mass., 1932), 355.

9. John Collier, *From Every Zenith: A Memoir and Some Essays on Life and Thought* (Denver, 1963), 106.

10. "Paso por Aqui!" *New Mexico Quarterly Review* 21 (Summer 1951):141.

11. *Theatre Arts* 9 (May 1925):301.

12. *Edge of Taos Desert*, 84.

13. *Lorenzo in Taos*, 20.

14. Tom Quirk and Robert E. Fleming, "Jean Toomer's Contributions to the *New Mexico Sentinel*," *College Language Association Journal* 19 (June 1976):531.

15. Claire Morrill, *A Taos Mosaic: Portrait of a New Mexican Village* (Albuquerque, N.M., 1973), 111.

16. Robinson Jeffers, *Selected Letters of Robinson Jeffers*, ed. Ann Ridgeway (Baltimore, 1968), 227, 230.

17. *Bookman*, 57 (July 1923):509–10.

18. Witter Bynner, *Journey With Genius* (New York, 1951), 336.

19. Reprinted in *Lorenzo in Taos,* 95–97.

20. Richard Cordell, "Becky Sharp," *Saturday Review* 24 (5 July 1941):10.

21. William Wasserstrom, "Phoenix on Turtle Island: D. H. Lawrence in Henry Adams' America," *Georgia Review* 32 (Spring 1978):172–97.

22. L. D. Clark, *The Dark Night of the Body* (Austin, 1964), 23.

23. *Saturday Review* 19 (26 November 1938):12–14.

24. *New York Times,* 28 February 1932, 4.

25. *Chicago Daily Tribune,* 20 February 1932, 14

26. In 1981 John Reed was portrayed by Warren Beatty as the hero of the film *Reds* for which Beatty also won an Oscar as director.

27. *Time* 28 (23 November 1936):91.

28. *Books,* 19 September 1937, 3.

29. "Taos Remembered: Recollections of a Time of Innocence," *American West* 8 (September 1971):40.

30. Donald Gallup, "The Mabel Dodge Luhan Papers," *Yale University Library Gazette* 37, no. 3 (January 1963):100.

Selected Bibliography

PRIMARY SOURCES

1. Books

Lorenzo in Taos. New York: Knopf, 1932.
Intimate Memories: Background. New York: Harcourt, 1933.
European Experiences. Vol. 2 of *Intimate Memories.* New York: Harcourt, 1935.
Winter in Taos. New York: Harcourt, 1935.
Movers and Shakers. Vol. 3 of *Intimate Memories.* New York: Harcourt, 1936.
Edge of Taos Desert: An Escape to Reality. Vol. 4 of *Intimate Memories.* New
    York: Harcourt, 1937.
Taos and Its Artists. New York: Duell, Sloan, 1947.

2. Articles, Essays, Poems, and Short Stories

(Poems are marked with an asterisk. A number of additional poems appear
    in *Lorenzo in Taos.*)

"Speculations." *Camera Work* (June 1913):6–9. Also published as "Specula-
    tions, or Post-Impressions in Prose," in *Arts and Decoration,* March
    1913.
*"My Beloved." *Mother Earth* 8, no. 2 (April 1913):55.
"The Secret of War." *Masses* 6, no. 2 (November 1914):8–9.
*"The Mirror." *Camera Work,* no. 47 (January 1915):9–11.
"A Quarrel." *Masses* 8, no. 11 (September 1916):16–17.
"The Parting." *Masses* 8, no. 12 (October 1916):8.
"The Eye of the Beholder." *Masses* 9, no. 12 (October 1917):10–11.
Syndicated column. *New York Journal* and other Hearst papers, 13 August
    1917–8 February 1918.
"Native Air." *New Republic* 42 (4 March 1925):40–42.
"A Bridge Between Cultures." *Theatre Arts Monthly* 9 (May 1925):297–301.
"Santos of New Mexico." *Arts* 7, no. 3 (1925):127–30.
"Southwest." *Dial* 79 (December 1925):477–84.
*"False Start." In *The Turquoise Trail,* edited by Alice C. Henderson. Bos-
    ton: Houghton, 1928, p. 93. Originally in *Poetry* 28 (June 1926):133.
"Georgia O'Keeffe in Taos." *Creative Arts* 8, no. 6 (1931):7–10.
"Taos—A Eulogy." *Creative Arts* 9, no. 4 (1931):289–95.

"Isadora Duncan." *New English Weekly* (Aug. 11, 1932):369–99.
"Lawrence of New Mexico." *New Mexico* 14, no. 2 (1936):9–11.
"Gowns by Adrian." *Town and Country* 91, no. 4 (1936):114–19.
"Holiday from Science?" *Southwest Review* 31 (Summer 1946):221–24.
"Paso por Aqui!" *New Mexico Quarterly* 21, no. 2 (Summer 1951):137–41.

3. Unpublished Works

Huntington Library. San Marino, California. Correspondence of Mary Austin and Carl Hovey.
University of California, Berkeley. Bancroft Library. Papers of D. H. Lawrence and of Una and Robinson Jeffers. Part of Mabel's story of the Jeffers was edited by Mark Shorer and published as *Una and Robin* (1976). Part of Mabel's account of the Jeffers is still restricted.
University of Texas, Austin. Humanities Research Center. Correspondence of D. H. and Frieda Lawrence and of Spud Johnson.
Yale University, New Haven, Connecticut. Beinecke Rare Book and Manuscript Library. The largest collection of Luhan material, as well as correspondence of Neith and Hutchins Hapgood, Leo Stein, Gertrude Stein, Alfred Stieglitz, and Spud Johnson. See Donald Gallup's "The Mabel Dodge Luhan Papers," *Yale University Library Gazette* 37, no. 3 (January 1963):97–105, for a summary of the holdings.
————. Sterling Library . Correspondence of John Collier.

SECONDARY SOURCES

Aaron, Daniel. *Writers on the Left: Episodes in American Literary Communism.* New York: Harcourt Brace, 1961. Mabel's "evenings," the Patterson strike pageant, the Armory art show.
Arnold, Armin. *D. H. Lawrence and America.* London: Linden, 1958. A rather uncomplimentary picture of Mabel in her relationship with Lawrence.
Austin, Mary. *Earth Horizon: An Autobiography.* Boston: Houghton Mifflin, 1932. Austin writes of their friendship during Mabel's years in Taos. Austin was living in Santa Fe and writing about the Indians.
Beagle, Peter S. "D. H. Lawrence in Taos." *Holiday* 42 (September 1967):45, 86–90. Taos in the 1960s and its past recalled by Dorothy Brett.
Benedict, Ruth. *Patterns of Culture.* New York: Houghton Mifflin, 1934. A long section concerns the culture of the Pueblo Indians, Tony Luhan's people.
Blanche, Jacques-Emile. *Aymeris.* Paris: Librairie Plan, 1923. A fictional portrait of Mabel as Giselle Links through the letters and diaries of the book's hero, Georges Aymeris.

————. *Portraits of a Lifetime.* Edited and translated by Walter Clement. New York: Coward-McCann, 1938. Blanche describes Mabel in Florence and his painting of several portraits of her.

Boyce, Neith. "Retreat." *Harper's Monthly* 146 (December 1922):46–66. A short story with a Mabel-like character in a sophisticated situation.

Brett, Dorothy. *Lawrence and Brett: A Friendship.* Philadelphia: Lippincott, 1933. Includes a present-tense account of Brett's relationship with Mabel and the Lawrences.

Brinig, Mryon. *All of Their Lives.* New York: Farrar, Straus, 1941. In this long novel Brinig makes use of Mabel's autobiographical volumes to create an egotistical, self-aggrandizing character.

Brinnin, John Malcolm. *The Third Rose: Gertrude Stein and Her World.* Boston: Little, Brown, 1959. Stein's life where it touches on Mabel's is part of Brinnin's story.

Bynner, Witter. *Cake, An Indulgence.* New York: Knopf, 1926. A short absurdist play satirizing a character based on Mabel. Reprinted in *The Works of Witter Bynner.* Edited by William Jay Smith. New York: Farrar, Straus, Giroux, 1978.

————. *Journey With Genius: Recollections and Reflections Concerning the D. H. Lawrences.* New York: John Day, 1951. Bynner records incidents from his association with Mabel during the years he lived in Santa Fe and traveled to Mexico with Lawrence.

Cantor, Milton. *Max Eastman.* New York: Twayne, 1970. Mabel's effect on Eastman was greater than their brief contacts would have foretold.

Carpenter, Frederick. *Robinson Jeffers.* New Haven: College and University Press, 1962. A survey of Jeffers's life and work includes mention of his association with Mabel.

"The Chicken Pull." *New Yorker* 21 (5 May 1945):17–18. An anonymous satirical interview.

Churchill, Allen. *The Improper Bohemians: The Re-Creation of Greenwich Village in Its Heyday.* New York: Dutton, 1959. A helpful characterization of the pre–World War I days in the Bohemia of Mabel's New York.

Clark, L. D. *The Dark Night of the Body: D. H. Lawrence's "The Plumed Serpent."* Austin: University of Texas Press, 1964. Kate in *The Plumed Serpent* is developed from Mabel, as Cipriano is from Tony Luhan.

Collier, John. *From Every Zenith: A Memoir and Some Essays on Life and Thought.* Denver: Sage, 1963. Collier describes his effort on behalf of the Indians and his association with Mabel in New York and Taos.

Cordell, Richard. "Becky Sharp, 1941." *Saturday Review* 24, no. 11 (5 July 1941):10. A review of Brinig's novel, *All of Their Lives.*

Cowan, James C. *D. H. Lawrence's American Journey.* Cleveland: Case Western Reserve Press, 1970. A fine study of how Lawrence's years in America affected his nature and his work.

Cowley, Malcolm. "Fable for Russian Children." *New Republic* 89 (25 November 1936):120, 122. Reprinted in Cowley's *Think Back on Us: A Contemporary Chronicle of the 1930's* (Carbondale: Southern Illinois University Press, 1967), 123–26. A humorous review of *Movers and Shakers*.

Davidson, Jo. *Between Sittings: An Informal Autobiography.* New York: Dial Press, 1951. Chapter 14, "In Italy with Mabel Dodge," concerns the sculptor's memories of Mabel and the Villa Curonia.

Draper, Muriel. *Music At Midnight.* New York: Harper, 1929. Draper details an incident with Mabel in Italy and reveals much about the life and times.

Eastman, Max. *Venture.* New York: Boni, 1927. Mabel and John Reed are models for the characters of Mary Kittridge and Jo Hancock in Eastman's novel.

————. *Enjoyment of Living.* New York: Harper, 1948. Eastman relates his association with Mabel in New York and Croton-on-Hudson.

Fergusson, Harvey. "Taos Remembered: Recollections of a Time of Innocence." *American West* 8 (September 1971):38–41. Fergusson, Southwest novelist and essayist, recalls Mabel, Tony, the Lawrences, and life in early Taos.

Foster, Joseph. *D. H. Lawrence in Taos.* Albuquerque: University of New Mexico Press, 1972. Foster, a young writer living in Taos at the time, gives his view of Mabel's affair with Lawrence, and Frieda's reaction.

Gallup, Donald, ed. *The Flowers of Friendship: Letters Written to Gertrude Stein.* New York, Knopf, 1953. Includes letters from Luhan to Stein.

————. "The Mabel Dodge Luhan Papers," *Yale University Library Gazette* 37, no. 3 (January 1963):97–105. Gallup describes the many letters and manuscripts housed in the Beinecke Library at Yale.

Goldman, Arnold. "The Culture of the Provincetown Players." *Journal of American Studies* 12, no. 3 (December 1978):291–310. Mabel played a part in the political and artistic factions on Cape Cod.

Gray, Madeline. *Margaret Sanger.* New York: Richard Marek, 1979. Mabel and Margaret Sanger influenced each other to believe that women should have the same sexual freedom as men.

Hahn, Emily. *Lorenzo: D. H. Lawrence and the Women Who Loved Him.* Philadelphia: Lippincott, 1975. Mabel's relationship to Lawrence is explored at length.

————. *Mabel: A Biography of Mabel Dodge Luhan.* Boston: Houghton Mifflin, 1977. An undocumented popularized story of Mabel's life based mainly on *Intimate Memories* and information supplied by her daughter-in-law.

Hapgood, Hutchins. *A Victorian in the Modern World.* New York: Harcourt, 1939. Intensive treatment of Mabel by a good friend.

Hicks, Granville. *John Reed: The Making of a Revolutionary.* New York: Macmillan, 1936. Includes Reed's affair with Mabel.

Hoffman, Frederick J. *Freudianism And The Literary Mind.* 2d ed. Baton Rouge: Louisiana State University Press, 1967. Mabel's use of psychiatrists and Lawrence's opinion of them are contrasted.

Homer, William Innes. *Alfred Stieglitz and the American Avant-Garde.* Boston: New York Graphic Society, 1977. Homer compares Mabel Dodge's salon to that of Stieglitz.

Hough, Graham. *The Dark Sun: A Study of D. H. Lawrence.* New York: Capricorn, 1959. Mabel figures in this biography of Lawrence as a model for several stories.

Jeffers, Robinson. *The Selected Letters of Robinson Jeffers 1897–1962.* Edited by Ann N. Ridgeway. Baltimore: Johns Hopkins Press, 1968. A number of letters concerning Mabel and Taos are included.

Kaplan, Justin. *Lincoln Steffens.* New York: Simon & Schuster, 1974. Kaplan details Steffens's relationship to Mabel and her salon.

Kellner, Bruce. *Carl Van Vechten and the Irreverent Decades.* Oklahoma City: University of Oklahoma Press, 1968. Mabel is fictionalized by Van Vechten and angered by his criticism of her work during their lengthy friendship.

Larson, Orville K. "Robert Edmond Jones, Gordon Craig and Mabel Dodge." *Theatre Research International* 3, no. 2 (February 1978):125 33. Because of Craig's antagonism to Mabel, he refused to see her protegé Jones.

Lasch, Christopher. *The New Radicalism in America 1889–1963: The Intellectual as a Social Type.* New York: Knopf, 1965. Extensive, critical treatment of Mabel and her life in New York.

Lawrence, D. H. *Phoenix: The Posthumous Papers of D. H. Lawrence.* Edited by Edward D. McDonald. New York: Viking, 1968. Three selections—"Taos," "New Mexico," and "Indians and an Englishman"—contain Lawrence's reaction to the climate, scenery, and Indians of New Mexico.

————. *St. Mawr and The Man Who Died.* New York: Vintage, 1952. In "St. Mawr" Mabel is fictionalized as Mrs. Witt, a bored, wealthy American woman living abroad and later in New Mexico with her daughter.

————. *Mornings in Mexico and Etruscan Places.* London: William Heinemann, 1956. Three selections—"The Hopi Snake Dance," "Indians and Entertainment," and "Dance of the Sprouting Corn"—were inspired by Lawrence's visits to the Indians of New Mexico.

————. *The Plumed Serpent.* New York: Vintage, 1959. Mabel and Tony furnish inspiration for characters in Lawrence's novel set in Mexico.

————. *The Complete Short Stories.* Vols. 2–3. New York: Viking, 1961.

"The Woman Who Rode Away" concerns a character suggested by Mabel's life, as do "The Princess" and "None of That."

————. *Collected Letters of D. H. Lawrence.* Edited by Harry Moore. New York: Viking, 1962. Lawrence writes to Mabel about a projected story of her life and to others about Mabel.

————. *Studies in Classic American Literature.* New York: Viking, 1964. After being brought to Taos by Mabel, Lawrence impressionistically evaluated the great works of American literature.

Lawrence, Frieda. *Frieda Lawrence: The Memoirs and Correspondence.* Edited by E. W. Tedlock. New York: Knopf, 1964. After Lawrence's death, Frieda corresponded with Mabel and returned to Taos.

————. *Not I But the Wind.* New York: Viking, 1934. Frieda's account of life in Taos.

Leuders, Edward. *Carl Van Vechten.* New York: Twayne, 1965. Mabel's friendship for Van Vechten enriches his life.

"Mabel's Comeback." *Time* 35 (22 January 1940):80. News stories on Mabel also appeared in *Time* 28 (23 November 1936):91 and 49 (5 May 1947):48.

"Mabel's Tony." *New Yorker* 15 (3 February 1940):14–15. Reprinted in Ely Jacques Kahn's *Far Flung and Footloose* (New York: Putnam, 1979). The Luhans visit New York City.

Mellow, James R. *Charmed Circle: Gertrude Stein and Company.* New York: Praeger, 1974. Mabel figures in several incidents in the life of Stein and Toklas.

Merrild, Knud. *With D. H. Lawrence in New Mexico.* London: Routledge & Kegan Paul, 1938. An account of Mabel from the view of a Danish painter who lived briefly on Lawrence's ranch.

"The Monumental Simplicity in the Pictorial Art of Maurice Sterne." *Current Opinion* 59 (December 1915):425–27. Quite a well-known painter before Mabel met him, Sterne's line drawings from Bali and one of Mabel are reproduced and praised.

Moore, Harry T. *The Intelligent Heart: The Story of D. H. Lawrence.* New York: Farrar Straus, 1954. Reprinted as *The Priest of Love: A Life of D. H. Lawrence* (1974). Mabel's influence is important in bringing Lawrence to America and on his writing when there.

Morrill, Claire. *A Taos Mosaic: Portrait of a New Mexican Village.* Albuquerque: University of New Mexico Press, 1973. Chapter 14, "Three Women of Taos," concerns Frieda Lawrence, Dorothy Brett, and Mabel Luhan.

Morris, Joe Alex. "Taos, New Mexico." *Saturday Evening Post* 223 (22 July 1950):22–23, 63, 66, 69. An historical account, including pictures of the town and of Mabel.

O'Connor, Richard. *The Lost Revolutionary: A biography of John Reed.* New York: Harcourt, 1967. Includes Mabel's love affair with Reed.

O'Neill, William. *The Last Romantic: A Life of Max Eastman.* New York: Oxford University Press, 1978. Mabel's life in Bohemia touches on Eastman's.

"Profiles." *New Yorker* 50, no. 2 (4 March, 1974):40–56. Mabel's relationship to painter Georgia O'Keeffe in Taos.

Rogers, W. G. *Ladies Bountiful.* New York: Harcourt, Brace, 1968, 106–35. Mabel figures in a large section of this volume on ladies who became the patrons of artists.

Roof, Stella J. "A Stranger in The World." *Saturday Review* 15 (21 Nov. 1936):7. A fair, well-written review of *Movers and Shakers.*

Rosenstone, Robert. *Romantic Revolutionary: A Biography of John Reed.* New York: Knopf, 1975. An older Mabel briefly loved a younger active seeker for a satisfying way of life.

Rubinstein, Arthur. *My Young Years.* New York: Knopf, 1973. The musician relates his visit to the Villa Curonia.

Rudnick, Lois Palken. "The Unexpurgated Self: A Critical Biography of Mabel Dodge Luhan." Ph.D. diss., Brown University, 1977. A well-documented study of the life and works of Luhan.

Sargeant, Elizabeth Shepley. "Sphynx of the Taos Desert." *Saturday Review* 19 (26 November 1938):12–14. A resident of Santa Fe and writer about the Indians gives an excellent, balanced analysis of Mabel's life work.

Skinner, Cornelia Otis. "Dithers and Jitters." In *Dithers and Jitters.* New York: Dodd, Mead, 1938, 3–7. Parodies *Movers and Shakers.*

Spacks, Patricia. *The Female Imagination.* New York: Knopf, 1975. An analysis of Mabel as biographer of her own life.

Spiel, Hilde. "Three Wise Ladies of Taos." *New Statesmen and Nation* 44, no. 1119 (16 August 1952):180–81. Mabel, Frieda Lawrence, and Dorothy Brett in Taos.

Steffens, Lincoln. *The Autobiography of Lincoln Steffens.* New York: Harcourt, 1931. A photograph of Mabel in this well-known account of the times illustrates the important place Steffens assigns to her life in New York.

Stein, Gertrude. *Selected Writings.* Edited by Carl Van Vechten, New York: Random, 1962. Includes "Portrait of Mabel Dodge at the Villa Curonia."

Stein, Leo. *Journey Into the Self.* Edited by Edmund Fuller. New York: Crown, 1950. Leo knew Mabel in Paris, Florence, Taos, New York City, and Croton-on-Hudson, and corresponded with her through the years.

Sterne, Maurice. *Shadow and Light: the Life, Friends and Opinions of Maurice Sterne.* Edited by Charlotte Leon Meyerson. New York: Harcourt, 1965. Sterne's view of his life with Mabel differs somewhat from hers in *Edge of Taos Desert.*

Tindall, William York. *D. H. Lawrence and Susan His Cow.* New York: Columbia University Press, 1939. An excellent study of Lawrence's relationship to nature through the cow he had on the ranch in Taos.

Toklas, Alice B. *The Letters of Alice B. Toklas.* Edited by Edward Burns. New York: Boni, 1973. As late as 1947 Toklas in a letter is still vitriolic in characterizing Mabel.

————. *What Is Remembered.* New York: Holt, Rinehart, 1963. Toklas remembers Mabel as rather ridiculous.

Trilling, Diana. *The Selected Letters of D. H. Lawrence.* New York: Farrar, Strauss, 1958. Lawrence's letters to Mabel and to his mother-in-law about Mabel are enlightening.

Van Vechten, Carl. *Peter Whiffle: His Life and Works.* New York: Knopf, 1922. As Edith Dale in this novel, Mabel's real life in Florence and New York is re-created.

————. "Ma Draper." *Yale University Library Gazette* 37, no. 4 (April 1963):125–29. Muriel Draper and Van Vechten knew Mabel at the Villa Curonia.

————. *Sacred and Profane Memories.* New York: Knopf, 1932. The author reviews his life of novel writing and people he has known.

————. "Some 'Literary Ladies' I have Known." *Yale University Library Gazette* 26, no. 3 (January 1952): 97–116. Pays tribute to Mabel.

Wasserstrom, William. "Phoenix on Turtle Island: D. H. Lawrence in Henry Adams' America." *Georgia Review* 32, no. 1 (Spring 1978):172–97. Mabel, who inspired "The Woman Who Rode Away," influenced Lawrence's attitude toward America.

Index

123

95986

CT
275
.L838
F7
1984

FRAZER, WINIFRED
 MABEL DODGE LUHAN.

DATE DUE

Fernald Library
Colby-Sawyer College
New London, New Hampshire

GAYLORD   PRINTED IN U.S.A.